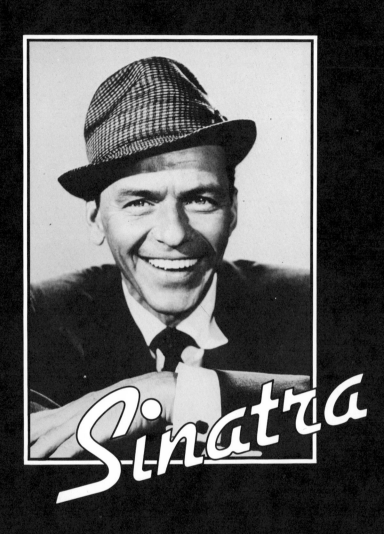

Sinatra

Alan Frank

Leon Amiel Publisher

New York

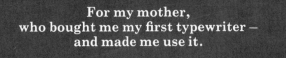

For my mother,
who bought me my first typewriter —
and made me use it.

Published by Leon Amiel Publisher
31 West 46th Street, New York, N.Y. 10036, U.S.A.

Library of Congress Catalog Card Number 78-55393
ISBN 0-8184-0700-3

Filmset in England by Photocomp Limited,
Birmingham
Printed in England by Butler and Tanner, Frome,
Somerset

Introduction

If there is one single factor which unites all aspects of show business, it is probably the almost universal dependence upon clichés. In the field of publicity, for instance, the use of cliché is all pervasive. Yet, despite this cynical over-use, and its (commonly) equally cynical acceptance, clichés are regarded as a means of making instant–and instantly comprehensible–contact with the public upon whose continuing goodwill and interest the whole of show business depends. In the majority of cases, the hyperbole of the publicist is seen as nothing more than a convenient shorthand in the process of creating new entertainers and consolidating their success. Thus, minimal research finds a plethora of 'overnight successes' who also vanished overnight, 'brilliant newcomers' who signally failed to survive their initial coming, and 'most promising actors or actresses' who faded without achieving stardom or even revealing just what it was that they were promising.

In order to succeed, it would appear that talent is helpful, as is luck. But in many cases the seeds of failure are sown when the performer is unable to meet the (minimal) requirements of the clichés of this profession. Even after success has been achieved, entertainers are still seen–and publicised–in terms of cliché. The 'rising star' becomes the 'star' and, when that over-used word loses its potency, he or she achieves the status of the 'superstar'. As each new superlative is brought into use, a fresher and more powerful one has to be found, and the ultimate weapon in a publicist's armoury is the phrase 'a legend in his/

The quintessential Sinatra—lean, wary, vulnerable

In August 1965, Sinatra joins the Hollywood immortals when he makes his palm prints in cement outside Grauman's Chinese Theatre (*below*), and (*right*) the screen Sinatra hoofs and sings with Gene Kelly in *Anchors Aweigh* (1945)

her own lifetime', one of the most abused tags around.

Like all clichés, it has been debased by constant and indiscriminate usage. The rise to the status of a 'legend' has become almost instantaneous, whereas the duration of a 'lifetime' has grown progressively shorter, thus largely rendering the expression meaningless. Few have been able even to measure up to the cliché, let alone the notion behind the phrase. Today, after the death of Bing Crosby, only Frank Sinatra survives as a genuine 'legend in his own lifetime'. That description was true twenty-five years ago, when Sinatra was once more the most powerful and successful entertainer in the world after one of the most sensational comebacks in the history of show business. The legend was unassailably there: today, a quarter of a century later, it has grown even greater.

Sinatra's private life has been lived so largely in the glare of the media's spotlights that much of what he has done and what has happened to him has achieved the status of myth. Despite his well-publicised love-hate relationship with the media, he has consistently used them to promote Sinatra the man as much as Sinatra the entertainer. In the process, inevitably facts have become distorted, fantasies have been made real by constant repetition: the legend is a tantalising mixture of the real and the mythical, in which there is no certainty of disentangling the strands.

In the immense coverage that has always been accorded to Sinatra's private life, it is often easy to forget that what he will ultimately be remembered for is not his brawls and his marriages, his romances and his constant hitting of the headlines, but his achievements as an artist. The legacy that Sinatra has already left to posterity is his recordings and his films, and it is these that will confirm his legendary status in the years to come when his headlines and his personal life are long forgotten. Sinatra himself would almost certainly

Supremely professional with a deceptively relaxed air, Sinatra at a recording session, ready to do take after take in search of the perfect fusion of music and lyrics

Onstage and in total command of
his material and his audience
(*right*), and (*opposite*) the 'Emperor
of Hollywood' relaxes with a
crossword puzzle

agree with this point of view. As long ago as 1951 he
told the pressmen, 'It wasn't the press who made me
famous. It was my singing.' That he then went on to add
'you miserable crumbs' merely serves to underline the
continuing 'hate' aspect of his relationship with the
media.

In telling the story of the kid from Hoboken who
rose, impelled by incredible ambition and self-
assurance, to become one of the most successful show-
business all-round entertainers, a tycoon and entrepreneur, as well as a man never far removed from world
headlines, I intend quite deliberately to concentrate
upon Sinatra the artist. Other facets of the man will
obviously emerge but in the legend that is Sinatra they
are ephemeral. In attempting to disentangle 'truth'
from 'legend', I have taken refuge on occasions in the
dictum propounded by James Stewart in John Ford's
film *The Man Who Shot Liberty Valance*: 'When truth
and legend conflict . . . print the legend.'

This then is Sinatra the artist, the man–and the
legend. All that remains is to quote singer Vic Damone:
'The man is a phenomenon. How can anyone do justice
to a legend?'

A Star is Born

T he small and grimy New Jersey town of Hoboken was an entirely unmemorable place in the year 1915. Covering about one square mile that fronted the Hudson River, Hoboken encompassed cobbled streets lined with frame houses and tenements, and the factories and the railroads which, with the docks and the shipyards, provided much of the town's employment. There was also one bar to every two hundred inhabitants.

Two years later, when America declared war on Germany on 6 April, 1917, Hoboken won brief eminence as the port of embarkation for American soldiers on their way to Europe to kill or be killed in the war to end all wars. That eminence was inevitably a transient one and Hoboken soon lapsed back into obscurity. But, on Sunday, 12 December, 1915, an event had taken place which was later to put Hoboken as surely on the show-business map as the small town of Plains, Georgia, has been placed on the political one.

♪ THE HOUSE I LIVE IN ♫

415 Monroe Street was a frame house shared by two families in what was a section of Hoboken predominantly inhabited by Italian-born Americans. Although everyday life there was punctuated by the ever-present dirt and noise of the Erie and Lackawanna railroads, the area was not, as would be maintained by publicists

opposite Ever dapper, Sinatra at three

below Sinatra (right, bottom row) at eight on vacation with family and friends in the Catskill Mountains. Dolly Sinatra sits behind him, holding a guitar

as late as 1952, a slum. According to Sinatra's uncle, Dominick Garaventi it was 'a pretty good lower-middle-class neighbourhood'.

Both Sinatra's parents, Anthony Martin Sinatra and Natalie Garaventi, had come to the United States as immigrants. His father had been born in Catania in Sicily whereas his mother, named Natalie because of her birth on Christmas Day, but known as Dolly, had come with her parents at the age of two months from Genoa.

Dolly was the first woman to have a profound effect upon the life of Frank Sinatra: she was also the undisputed driving force behind her family, a fact accepted and acknowledged without rancour by her husband. Today, when Women's Liberation is as fashionable as it is operative, a woman like Dolly Sinatra would be pre-eminent. Her power and dominance in local politics in Hoboken during Frank Sinatra's

formative early years are all the more remarkable since her achievements were carried through in a period when the woman's role was generally accepted as being one that was totally submissive.

At the time of Frank Sinatra's birth, his father was working as a boilermaker in the Hoboken shipyards, having previously had an undistinguished career as a bantamweight boxer who never made it beyond local semi-finals and who had fought under the name of Marty O'Brien. (An Irish name was considered a prerequisite if a boxer was to pull in the crowds, and Sinatra's blue eyes made his acceptance as an Irishman a simple matter.) When he lost his job at the shipyards, Dolly took complete charge of her husband's career. Borrowing the money from her mother, she bought him a tavern and often worked there as a barmaid. Later, as her influence and power in

Dolly and Frank pose beside the family automobile in
the late Twenties, their close relationship already
evident

local politics grew, she was able to obtain for
him a post in the Hoboken Fire Department.
Eventually, Anthony Martin Sinatra worked
his way up to the rank of captain, by which title
he was referred to until his death in 1969.

♫WHY WAS I BORN?♫

His parents had been married for just over six
years when Francis Albert Sinatra was born in
the cold-frame house in December 1915. The
birth was an extremely difficult one. Young
Sinatra weighed an incredible thirteen and a
half pounds and, in the course of a complicated
forceps delivery, the doctor was unable to avoid
damaging part of the child's head and neck, as
well as nearly severing an ear lobe. The scars
have stayed: years later Sinatra was to refuse
the requests of movie-studio executives to have
them cosmetically removed. But the lacera-

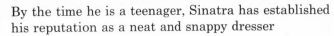
tions were only part of Sinatra's birth trauma. The attending doctor was heard to say, 'I don't think he'll live, so let's take care of the mother.' Not for the last time in his life, Sinatra was being written off prematurely. But his maternal grandmother, Rosa Garaventi, ignored the doctor and held the apparently stillborn child under water from the cold tap: the physical shock made him breathe.

Although later publicity was often to stress unhappy elements in Sinatra's childhood, like so much that has been written about him, it has become an almost impossible task to separate the myths and legends from the reality and facts. Certainly, as the only child, young Frank was spoiled by Dolly and given a large amount

of love during those periods when she was able to spend time with her son. That those periods were relatively sparse was inevitable, since a few years after the birth of her son Dolly embarked upon her career in local politics.

Working at her husband's tavern as a barmaid had never been more than a stop-gap for Dolly Sinatra, although it taught her much about people and politics since the saloons were the natural breeding grounds for social and political thought. She trained as a nurse and began to channel that training into helping the wives and families of the local Hoboken workers. Soon she became known as a local Lady Bountiful, a fixer who could be relied upon to help people with their problems. She understood people, both those who needed aid and those who were in a position to give it. She had an almost axiomatic response to every problem, one that usually worked: 'Let's fight this at City Hall.'

City Hall in Hoboken was run by the Democratic Party. Indeed all Hudson County, of which Hoboken was a part, was run for the Democrats by the ruthless and corrupt political boss, Frank Hague, mayor of New Jersey. As her success as a negotiator became more and more evident, Dolly was appointed a district leader for the Democratic Party and she could always be relied upon to deliver her guaranteed quota of votes for the Democratic candidate at election times.

With much of Dolly's time taken up in politics, Frank's early upbringing was seen to by his maternal grandmother. He also spent time with his erstwhile baby-sitter, Mrs Rosa Carrier, who had lived in the house opposite the Sinatras'. Later on, after the death of his grandmother, Sinatra was to find another part-time mother, this time an elderly Jewish woman called Mrs Goldberg. But despite this apparently fragmented upbringing, Sinatra did learn much from both parents, and their influence was to crystallise into some of his more obvious latter-day traits.

Dolly Sinatra equated dirt with poverty, and Sinatra's sometimes almost obsessional habits of personal cleanliness and neatness clearly stem from his mother's credo. From her, too, he learned respect for achievements gained through hard work. She also imbued in him a fighting spirit, and this, allied to the fiery temper and emotional volatility he had inherited from her, lies behind many of his adult attitudes and actions. Dolly doted upon her only son, giving him an ample allowance and seeing to it that he was the best dressed boy on the block. That attention to dress, which Sinatra was to inherit, had started early. Dolly once said, 'I wanted a girl and I bought a lot of pink clothes. When Frank was born, I didn't care. I dressed him in pink, anyway.' Later the pink gave way to Little Lord Fauntleroy suits, which in turn gave way to the neat, well-dressed Sinatra who earned for himself the nickname of 'Slacksy' because he owned so many pairs of trousers.

'The only man in town I'd be afraid to fight is Sinatra. I might knock him down but he'd keep getting up until one of us was dead . . .'

ROBERT MITCHUM

That elegance in dress and the reputed wardrobe of suits, trousers, and jackets would have been the envy of any man, let alone the other kids with whom Frank mixed at school and after. So it was more than fortunate that by the time he was ten, the skinny-looking Sinatra had been discovered by neighbourhood children older than himself to be a formidable opponent in a fight. Dolly told him, 'Go fight your own battles', and his father and uncle Dominick Garaventi, who had once been a professional boxer under the name of Babe Sieger, made sure that the youngster learned how to handle himself in a fight. He may have looked different from his fellows, but he was soon known to be a slugger. The Fighting Frank whose battles would one day become headlines was already formed. Then, as later, no-one tangled too often with Frank Sinatra. As a child, he was involved in plenty of fights, partly because of his temper, partly because he was Italian-American in an ethnic melting-pot, and partly because fighting was a way of life in Hoboken. But he never backed down or became a bully.

His reputation as a fearless and powerful fighter against racial intolerance stems from those early days. Yet his later battles were often to be misunderstood and misinterpreted, winning him enemies rather than friends, and antagonistic headlines instead of plaudits. He has recalled the origins of many of these violent latter-day outbursts: 'I lived in a plenty tough neighbourhood. When somebody called me a "dirty little Guinea", there was only one thing to do–break his head. When I got older, I realised that you shouldn't do it that way. I realised that you've got to do it through education. Children are not to blame. It is the parents. How can a child know whether his playmate is an Italian, a Jew or Irish, unless the parents have discussed it in the privacy of their homes. They hear their parents talk . . . and they must think that there is something wrong with being a Catholic or a Jew.' Years later, in Hollywood, that philosophy was to bear fruit in the short *The House I live In* which Sinatra made with Mervyn LeRoy, a film which dealt realistically with the then practically taboo subject of racial intolerance.

Later the Sinatras moved from the house in

How Deep Is The Ocean? Sinatra and Gene Kelly as sailors on furlough in the 1945 MGM movie *Anchors Aweigh*

Monroe Street to better and well-maintained homes on Madison Street and Hudson Street. By the time he was a teenager, Sinatra already had a charge account at the town's only department store and his generosity with money and with gifts of clothes to his less fortunate friends–another trait that was to carry over into his adult life–had become established. At sixteen he was able to run his own car, a somewhat beat-up second-hand Chrysler.

Growing up in an Italian community, with family gatherings, Sinatra absorbed the music that formed an integral part of Italian weddings and celebrations. So it was hardly surprising that he should become interested in music or see in show business a way out of the greyness and soullessness of Hoboken. Long before he reached his teens, Sinatra was collecting the records of singers such as Rudy Vallee and his real idol, Bing Crosby, and decorating the walls of his bedroom with their photographs. A life characterised by the tension and aggression of a racially mixed environment, where the only way to avenge an insult was to use one's fists, held no attraction for Sinatra.

♫ MY GIRL ♫

When he was about fifteen, his uncle Dominick Garaventi gave him a ukelele: that year he met the dark and attractive Nancy Barbato and the ukelele was employed to serenade Nancy. The only kid in the neighbourhood who played a musical instrument, Sinatra would sit under the lamp post in front of his house while Nancy and the others listened to him imitate Crosby and another singing idol, Russ Columbo. He joined up with a teenage band and they got the odd date, playing at a wedding celebration or for an anniversary party. At that time, Sinatra was more interested in his ukelele than in his singing. But this was to change, a year before he quit high school.

By then he was going steady with Nancy Barbato and in March 1933 he and Nancy went to see Bing Crosby, in person on the stage of a vaudeville theatre in Jersey City. The experience was the catalyst he had needed. He told Nancy, 'I'm going to be a singer', and he repeated this ambition when he returned home that evening. Legend has it that Dolly threw a shoe at a picture of Crosby in her son's room while, according to Sinatra, his father 'thought that anyone who wanted to go into the music business must be a bum'. Nevertheless, the next time Sinatra performed with the teenage band, it was as a singer–the ukelele had gone for ever.

Despite Dolly's determination that Sinatra should have a good education, his time at school was relatively brief and undistinguished. He went to the David E. Rue Junior High School and then on to Demarest High. His schooling there lasted only forty-seven days, after which he dropped out. Later, Sinatra was to express regret that his formal education had been so brief. He was quoted as saying: 'There are several things I think I would have done if I had the chance again. I would have been a little more patient about getting out into the world. I would have seen to it that I had a more formal education. I would have become an accomplished musician, in the sense that I would have studied formally, even if I never used it.'

Having left school, parental pressure forced Sinatra to enrol–albeit briefly–for courses at the Stevens Institute of Technology while working for the *Jersey Observer*. At first he loaded newspapers onto trucks and later had the less physically demanding job of a copy boy. Neither the job nor the courses lasted long: already sporting plaid jackets similar to those worn by Crosby, Sinatra quit to become a singer, set on defying Dolly, if necessary.

Dolly still disapproved of her son's choice of profession. But she supported him once it became clear that he was not to be weaned away from that choice. She bought, for $65, a portable amplifier and microphone which stowed away into a rhinestone-studded case and began to use her political influence to get him singing jobs in the roadhouses that had sprung up all over New Jersey with the ending of Prohibition.

Sinatra, too, flung himself into his career with what amounted to something of an obsessive determination to make it to the top. It

Images: Sinatra's singing idol, Bing Crosby (*below*), and the teenage Frank emulates Crosby, hair parted and pipe in hand (*left*)

was a determination compounded of a desire to prove to his parents that his decision had been the right one and the fierce self-esteem that had been instilled into him during his upbringing as an Italian-American, an upbringing in which the concept of pride was one of the paramount factors–pride in oneself, one's background, and one's achievements.

♪NICE WORK IF YOU CAN GET IT♪

Sinatra sang at every venue and occasion he could–not just in New Jersey roadhouses but in every amateur talent contest held in vaudeville theatres in New York, Newark, Jersey City, and in Hoboken itself. It was as winner of an amateur contest at the State Theater in Jersey City that Sinatra got the chance to appear as a contestant in the more important competition at the Academy of Music on 14th Street in New York. Later, Sinatra was to recall the occasion: 'I'm standing there shaking, figuring that the moment they announce a guy from Hoboken, he's dead!' He was wrong. He did well enough, though he failed to win the contest. He returned to the grind of one-night performances, always improving and waiting for the big break.

He had one basic theory: 'Stay alive, stay active, and get as much practice as you can.' It was a theory that was to pay off. By 1935, Sinatra would be a professional entertainer, his apprentice period over. From then on, it becomes the story of Sinatra the performer, as much as the man.

Enter 'The Voice'

Today, for the aspiring singing star, show business offers all the short-cuts open in a situation where the business aspect usually predominates. The media, too, are more pervasive now, and a single television appearance can turn an unknown into a 'star'—although exposure on that same medium can just as easily reverse the process, particularly when the star is a product more of economics and promotion than of talent.

In the Thirties, however, none of these short-cuts was open to Sinatra. 'Overnight' success then was a slow and gruelling process of song plugging, one-night stands, and longer night-club engagements, along with any radio work, paid or unpaid, that came along. Anything, in fact, that could get a singer started on the one 'sure' way to stardom as a solo performer—becoming a singer with one of the big-name bands.

This was the era of the Big Bands; with their famous leaders they were the current stars of popular music. Sinatra knew that he would have to follow the example of his idol, Bing Crosby, who had begun as a singer with the Paul Whiteman orchestra. Even though the vocalists were subordinated to the star image of the Big Bands and their leaders, being used as just another 'instrument' in the orchestra, they gained valuable experience and exposure on nationwide tours, in front of live audiences and over local radio links. And there were the opportunities offered as vocalist on the band's records followed by, hopefully, success as a solo vocalist, recording contracts, and finally, juke-box stardom.

♪HIGH HOPES♩

Sinatra began his grind towards the initial goal of becoming a band singer with only a driving ambition and a determination to gain as much experience as possible. He grabbed at every chance to sing, more for the experience than for the money it paid. He even took an unpaid job on a local radio station, a job obtained for him through his uncle Dominick's political contacts. Finally, his 'break' came.

At that time one of the best opportunities for a 'local' talent to be discovered was the radio show known as 'Major Bowes Amateur Hour'. It was a talent contest but one that was totally different from all the local contests which Sinatra had been entering. Firstly, it was recognised as a legitimate career stepping-stone to appear on the show, and secondly, since the show was broadcast from New York, it offered the singer the chance to be heard by a much larger audience—and be judged by them.

Sinatra wrote for an audition and was accepted. He turned up for his audition at the same time as a trio of singers cum instrumentalists who also came from Hoboken. They too were accepted and Major Bowes apparently teamed the quartet as the Hoboken Four. On 8 September, 1935, with Frank Sinatra as the lead singer, the Hoboken Four appeared on 'Major Bowes Amateur Hour', which was broadcast live from the stage of New York's Capitol Theater. The audience in the theatre—and over the air—liked what they heard. The meter which measured the applause and the tele-

phone callers who rang Murray Hill 8-9983 gave first prize to the Hoboken Four. That was to be Sinatra's last performance as an amateur. First prize on the show was the chance to become members of one of Major Bowes's travelling units, troupes that toured the country playing to local audiences. Sinatra and the others received $50 a week, plus their meals.

Sinatra only stayed with the unit for a few months. It became obvious as the tour progressed that Sinatra was the star of the Hoboken Four, and the other three members were inevitably forced into the role of a supporting group. There was mounting dissension and finally fights among the Four. At Oakland in California, Sinatra sang with a nightclub orchestra at the request of its leader: the audience response to a performance that

was given without even a rehearsal was to refuse to let him leave the stage. Even before that, it was Sinatra who was being mobbed backstage after the shows: the skinny singer was already demonstrating his incredible sex appeal. Sinatra, realising that working with the Major Bowes unit was no way to attain the success he wanted, quit and returned to Hoboken. He now knew something of the power and appeal he possessed. All that was needed was a way to deploy that talent.

Once again, it was Dolly who helped. Sinatra returned to his one-night stands with his microphone and amplifier and now work with the clubs and roadhouses seemed easier to obtain. More experience, but not in the direction Sinatra wanted to go. If he was to make it as a singer, he had to become a vocalist with a name band. Dolly began by using her influence to get her son a steady job, singing at the Union, a local club, for $40 a week. But the consuming ambition that impelled him didn't stop there. By the early part of 1938, Sinatra was singing on no fewer than eighteen radio shows, for five local radio stations in New York and New Jersey. It wasn't the money—he never received payment from any of the stations, except the Mutual Broadcasting System, which gave him an allowance to travel to the studios. Sinatra was willingly giving his talent for nothing, in return for the exposure that he needed.

More legend. Some sources credit Dolly with giving Sinatra his next break by using her influence to get him a job with the New Jersey roadhouse, the Rustic Cabin, situated near Englewood. Sinatra himself wrote in *American Weekly*: 'I got my job when some musician friends brought me to Harold Arlen, then bandleader at the Cabin. Arlen gave me my first chance for $15 a week. . . .' Whatever brought Sinatra to the Rustic Cabin, the reason behind the move despite its dramatic drop in salary from his $40 a week at the Union Club was obvious. Unlike the Union Club, the Rustic Cabin was wired to broadcast live over radio station WNEW. That meant additional—and regular—exposure, and Sinatra's decision was to be amply justified. However, his job at the Cabin was no sinecure. True, he sang with the Harold Arlen band, with a group called the Three Pages—but he also had to act as a master of ceremonies and wait at tables.

♪ LOVE AND MARRIAGE ♪

Although she must have known that his first thoughts would always be for his career, on 4 February, 1939, Nancy Barbato married her childhood sweetheart at Our Lady of Sorrows Church in Jersey City. Sinatra's weekly salary at the Rustic Cabin had been raised to $25 a week shortly before the marriage and his parents gave the newlyweds a black Chrysler. In it they drove through the state of North Carolina on a four-day honeymoon, returning to live in a $42 a month three-room apartment at 487 Garfield Avenue, Jersey City. Nancy took a job as a secretary to help out financially. It meant that she worked days while her husband worked nights, but Frank had what he wanted— a regular, five day a week radio outlet for his

work, albeit only locally, over station WNEW.

In June 1939, the hoped-for major breakthrough arrived, at a time when the Sinatras' financial and emotional fortunes were at low ebb. Star trumpeter Harry James, once himself 'discovered' by 'King of Swing' Benny Goodman in whose orchestra he had played, himself 'found' Frank Sinatra. James had left the Goodman orchestra in February 1939 to form his own band, mostly with money lent to him by Goodman himself. One night he was in bed, listening to 'Dance Parade' on radio station WNEW. He heard a singer, but did not catch his

above left Sinatra's last disc with Harry James was cut in Hollywood on 8 November, 1939

above right Bandleader as star: Harry James, 'Idol of Jitterbugs'

left Big Band Days. Harry James and his orchestra on the set of the 1943 Lucille Ball movie *Best Foot Forward* with vocalist Helen Forrest on the left

25

name, only the name and location of the Rustic Cabin. The next night James turned up to hear Sinatra in person. He liked what he heard, particularly the singer's way of handling a lyric. Sinatra was signed to a two-year contract with the Harry James band, at a salary of $75 a week. It wasn't the name band that Sinatra had been hoping for, but it was the breakthrough he wanted, something he could turn to his own advantage. Jubilantly, Sinatra telephoned Nancy: 'I told her to quit her job. She was going to travel on the road with me and Harry James!'

Sinatra and James got on well together, once Sinatra had made it quite clear to the band leader that he was not going to change his name. He had fought too long for that name already. Sinatra liked James's straightforward manner and James's circus background appeared to fit in with Sinatra's tough early days in Hoboken. As for James, he was quoted as saying that the singer 'fit right into the band. He got along beautifully with all the guys.'

Nancy was there to give Sinatra support when he made his first appearance with the band at Baltimore's Hippodrome Theater. It was the last week in June 1939. Sinatra sang two numbers, 'My Love For You' and 'Wishing'. Since this was real life and not the movies, the world did not shake. But neither did Sinatra: he took fronting a big band in his stride with the one commodity he was never to lack in his life — supreme self-confidence. It was another step towards his goal of really big-time stardom. Much of his childhood ambition had come true: the rest should be only a matter of time.

The band returned from Baltimore to New York, where it played during the 1939 World's Fair at Roseland. It was here that Sinatra first revealed his hunger for media recognition. It was a hunger that was to turn in later years into a powerful love-hate relationship with the media. When he needed them, they had not always been there: when, like Garbo, he wanted to be left alone, he was too big a story for the media to ignore.

♪ THE IMPATIENT YEARS ♫

But in 1939 Sinatra *had* to have publicity. He convinced the band's manager of this and, in turn, manager Gerry Barrett persuaded music critic George T. Simon — who had come to write about the band — to mention its singer as well.

'This boy,' said Barrett, 'wants a good write-up more than anybody I've ever seen.' He got it, in an article in *Metronome* which mentioned 'the very pleasing vocals of Frank Sinatra, whose easy phrasing is especially commendable'. The review may have been written under pressure, but in its content it shows remarkable foreknowledge of the singer Sinatra was to become. And, if on that occasion Sinatra had to beg for a mention, the reverse was also true. It was reported in *Down Beat* that Harry James once asked a reporter to soft pedal his praise for the singer. James was quoted as saying, 'If he hears you compliment him, he'll demand a raise tonight!'

'His name is Sinatra, and he considers himself the greatest vocalist in the business. Get that! No one's even heard of him! He's never had a hit record, and he looks like a wet rag, but he says he's the greatest.'

HARRY JAMES

Sinatra was yet to become the greatest singer in the world, but already, as far as the public was concerned, he was on his way. Just as on the ill-fated Major Bowes unit tour, his sex appeal was getting to the females in the audiences. And fast. Connie Haines, the female vocalist with the band, recalled, 'Our first booking after he joined us was the Hippodrome in Baltimore. Frank was so new he wasn't even billed. The fans didn't know his name but nevertheless they were standing at the stage door, screaming and yelling for him.' The legendary Sinatra, the crooner who would reduce a whole generation of bobbysoxers to hysteria, was beginning to emerge.

Sinatra was imbued with an immense self-confidence which often manifested itself as cockiness. But behind the cockiness, he was impatient and worried about the relative lack of progress of the James band. After their stint at Roseland, and a brief period playing in Atlantic City, they headed west, playing in Chicago before going on to Los Angeles and disaster.

James himself was still extremely popular and was voted the Number One trumpeter in the *Down Beat* annual poll for 1939: his orchestra, however, could only come in at Number Twelve among the big bands. Clearly, James was not

going to repeat the success of the Benny Goodman orchestra. Los Angeles and the smart dining spot, Victor Hugo's in Hollywood's Beverley Hills, saw to that. James had been forced to accept the booking when they reached Los Angeles only to find that their original venue, the famous Palomar Ballroom, had burned down. The 'in' people who came to Victor Hugo's to dine and dance failed completely to appreciate the brassy sound of the James band. The management, faced with declining attendances, agreed that the band's music was at odds with the classy atmosphere normally associated with Victor Hugo's. They fired them, refusing to pay a cent.

For the James band, the fiasco at Victor Hugo's meant financial as well as artistic disaster. James was forced to release Connie Haines as the band headed east again. By then, Nancy Sinatra was no longer travelling with them. Learning that she was pregnant, Sinatra sent her home to New Jersey to prepare for the birth of their first child.

James managed to get a booking at the

Panther Room in Chicago's Sherman Hotel. It was only some six months since he had employed Sinatra on a two-year contract. It is a measure of Harry James, the man, that when, at the start of 1940, his star vocalist was offered a job with the top-lining Tommy Dorsey Orchestra, he refused to stand in his way, despite the valid contract. He urged Sinatra to accept Dorsey's offer, dissolving their contract with a handshake. 'I never did get around to tearing up the contract,' he is quoted as saying. 'But Nancy was expecting a baby and Frank needed the money, and I wasn't going to stand in his way.'

The Tommy Dorsey Orchestra was then among the top bands in the States. At the time the James band arrived in Chicago, the Dorsey Orchestra was playing down the street from the Sherman Hotel, at the Palmer House. Various versions, all equally convincing, or unconvincing, depending upon how you like your legends proffered, exist to explain how Tommy Dorsey came to offer Sinatra a job. Each version has a different person being credited with bringing the singer's talents to Dorsey's attention. What is certain is that Dorsey was already looking for a replacement for his lead singer, the temperamental Jack Leonard. Whoever–or whatever–was the catalyst that brought Dorsey and Sinatra together, the result was what Sinatra had so desperately wanted– the chance to sing with a really big name band. Only Glenn Miller could be considered a rival to Dorsey, and Dorsey's band was considered the singer's band because Miller's arrangements tended always to favour the orchestra at the expense of the vocalist.

Sinatra had to swallow his pride in gaining the Dorsey job. For his audition at the Palmer House he was on trial to see just how well he could imitate Jack Leonard and his famous rendition of 'Marie'. For Sinatra, with his already evolving style and phrasing, it must have been a galling experience. Nonetheless, he went along with what he was asked to do and was hired, at a salary of $100 a week.

On 26 January, 1940, Sinatra sang for the last time with the James band. He was entering a new phase in his career and clearly the parting affected him. In his own words, he described the end of the James era. 'That night the bus pulled out with the rest of the boys. I'd said goodbye to them all, and I remember it was snowing. There was nobody around, and I stood alone with my suitcase in the snow, and watched the tail-lights disappear. Then the tears started, and I tried to run after the bus.'

Although Sinatra had been singing with the Harry James band for only a few months, he was no mere novice, as his selection as the replacement for the highly popular Jack Leonard had proved. That he had achieved his first major career goal and become a singer with the country's biggest band was proof to Sinatra that his belief in his talent was not misplaced. Looking to the future, there was no bigger or better band he could aspire to join. What he could do was use the time he was to spend with Dorsey gaining experience and refining and amplifying his talent ready for the next major step in his career. Once he had conquered the world of the Big Bands, he could turn his energies towards becoming a solo performer and challenge Crosby in his own territory.

At that time, the Dorsey Orchestra contained some of the most talented musicians then working in the Big Bands–a roster that included Bunny Berrigan, Joe Bushkin, Ziggy Elman, and drummer Buddy Rich. The latter was the possessor of a temper and ego matched only by Tommy Dorsey–and Sinatra himself.

He was soon accepted as one of the band, although there was never to be the easy-going cameraderie that had characterised the days

with Harry James. Said Jo Stafford, the female member of Dorsey's singing group, the Pied Pipers, 'He was very well liked in the band and he certainly worked hard to fit in.' In fact, he fitted in because he was already a true professional, always working to improve when he was off stage and giving his songs all that he had to give in performance.

It was with the Dorsey band that Sinatra's easy way with money, a trait that had begun as a kid in Hoboken, really took root. It was always Sinatra who picked up the tab, who was the generous one. Then again, his personal cleanliness impressed his fellow band-members. Despite the travelling conditions and the one-night stands, he was always clean and smartly groomed. His trousers always held a crease, his dress was always immaculate. His insistence upon personal hygiene became something of a

joke, leading to such remarks as 'You know, he changes his shirt every day' and 'Can you believe that guy? He won't eat off a dirty plate!'

But, in addition to these positive attributes, the Dorsey years also earned for Sinatra a reputation for bad temper and sudden flashes of violence. In the process of finding himself as an entertainer, Sinatra was also establishing some of the less likeable traits that were to characterise his later life and career.

♪WANDERING♫

The Dorsey Orchestra was a hard training-ground and the outbursts of temper and violence were the almost inevitable result of a non-stop sequence of major engagements, punctuated by a gruelling series of one-night stands between the bigger shows. The band toured the

country by bus, playing in the evenings, then travelling through the night, fighting for sleep, and on through the next day, to the evening engagement. There were times when their schedule meant as many as nine shows a day: for Sinatra, the singer, that could mean twelve songs. Then there was radio work and recording dates.

Sinatra was gaining the experience and the exposure he wanted, but at a price. In his work, it showed in incidents such as the time drummer Buddy Rich interrupted one of Sinatra's songs for a solo passage of his own: Sinatra hurled a glass at him. Again, on an occasion when one of the audience in Omaha threw popcorn at Jo Stafford, Sinatra hurtled off the bandstand into the audience, looking for the man: fortunately, he didn't spot him, since he was ready to 'tear him to pieces'.

The pressure of performing at such a pitch also took a heavy toll on Sinatra's personal life. When he was able to return home to New Jersey between engagements, he found himself matching its tranquillity with nervous and edgy behaviour. Already his marriage was beginning to crumble. It had perhaps survived so long because of their proximity when the two of them had been on the road together with Harry James. In his travels with the Dorsey orchestra, Sinatra was inevitably meeting smart, sophisticated, and rich women and comparing them with the simplicity and gentleness of Nancy. He was in the process of becoming a show-business 'personality', whereas Nancy remained basically the same as she had always been. It was a recipe for ultimate marital disaster.

On 8 June, 1940, Sinatra's first child, Nancy Sandra Sinatra, was born: he had been singing with the band at New York's Astor Roof but had been too tired to make the trip back to his home in New Jersey. It was a telephone call from the Margaret Hague Hospital in Jersey City that told him he was a father.

At twenty-four, Sinatra seemed to have everything going for him. The song 'I'll Never Smile Again', sung by Sinatra and accompanied by the Pied Pipers and the Dorsey Orchestra, was a hit. And that June, the orchestra became the regular summer replacement for the Bob Hope radio show, giving Sinatra further experience, further exposure. The money was coming in and, true to form, was being spent almost as fast.

By October 1940, the band had their own radio show. That month they also made the trip to Hollywood to open the Palladium Ballroom. Sinatra liked the flash and glamour of Hollywood and returned there in 1941 to feature as the vocalist in the Tommy Dorsey Orchestra's appearance in a low-budget Paramount musical called *Las Vegas Nights*. He sang his hit song 'I'll Never Smile Again': *Metronome*'s George T. Simon was slightly less enthusiastic than he had been when writing about Sinatra in his Harry James days, saying that, 'He sings prettily in an unphotogenic manner.' Still, that was a better review than Simon gave to *Las Vegas Nights* as a whole.

Sinatra's career with Dorsey lasted until 2 July, 1942. During that time the singer, who had had but five recording sessions while with the Harry James band, made over ninety records, establishing himself as a major recording star. To Jo Stafford, it was clearly inevitable. Recalling Sinatra's first appearance with the orchestra at Rockford, Illinois, at the end of January 1940, Jo Stafford has been quoted as saying, 'We were onstage when Tommy announced Frank's first appearance. As Frank came up to the mike I just thought, "Hmmmm—kinda thin". But by the end of the eight bars, I was thinking, "This

is the greatest sound I've ever heard." But he had more. Call it talent. You knew he couldn't do a number badly.' By the time Sinatra became a solo performer, Jo Stafford's intuitive first impressions had been more than confirmed. Sinatra had learned and worked and practised until his voice was no longer merely accompanied by the orchestra—it was a new and beautiful solo instrument, under the control of a master.

The parting from Dorsey, when it came, was not to be with the good wishes and the handshake that had characterised the break with Harry James. Instead, it would be bitter and acrimonious. That that parting had to come, sooner rather than later, was inevitable. The same talent that Dorsey had seen in the skinny kid he hired to replace Jack Leonard was becoming more controlled, and Sinatra's continual striving for improvement was getting noticed, by the public, by the music publishers and the song pluggers, and by the media. As far as the volatile and egoistic Dorsey was concerned, his orchestra had only one star—Dorsey himself. But events were robbing him of this status and as Sinatra's appeal increased, so did the friction between the two. Clearly the departure of the singer could only be a matter of time.

The signs had been visible for some while. When Sinatra sang, couples would stop dancing and crowd around the bandstand to listen. Sinatra, too, was aware of his effect upon audiences and was using that power, his self-confidence growing with every performance. His abilities and talents were now outgrowing the job of a band singer, however prestigious that band might be.

The success of Sinatra's recordings with the band—numbers such as 'Stardust', 'Whispering', 'The One I Love' and 'Let's Get Away From It All'—served to underline his appeal. It was good news in one sense for Dorsey, but it also

meant that the spotlight, due to him as the leader of the band, was shifting onto his vocalist.

♪ I'M GONNA MAKE IT ALL THE WAY ♪

By 1942, it was clear that Sinatra had become the main attraction. The first sign had been the result of the poll carried out by *Billboard* in their annual survey of college students' musical tastes: in May 1941, Sinatra was named as Number One male vocalist. At the end of that year, Sinatra had overtaken Bing Crosby and was named by *Down Beat* as the Most Outstanding Male Band Vocalist in the United States, a position that had been held by Crosby from 1937 to 1940. Then, in January 1942, the readers of *Metronome* voted Sinatra the Best Male Band Singer for 1941.

If the magazine polls were good news for Sinatra–whose songs were getting well aired on radio and on the nation's jukeboxes–they were less pleasant reading for Dorsey. The same *Down Beat* poll that lauded Sinatra placed the Dorsey band at Number Two to Benny Goodman in the Swing Bands and Number Two in the Sweet Bands to Glenn Miller, while as a solo performer Dorsey was placed below Artie Shaw, Harry James, and Goodman.

Then, even more significantly, instead of approaching Dorsey first, song pluggers began offering their wares directly to Sinatra. The press, too, gravitated towards the singer, his popular success having made him in their eyes the most important member of the Dorsey outfit–and that included Dorsey himself. Axel Stordahl, then one of Dorsey's arrangers and later to become Sinatra's own musical director, summed it up neatly when he was quoted as saying, 'It was not Tommy's show, but Frank's.'

Finally, under pressure from his own record label, Dorsey was forced to satisfy popular demand and let Sinatra make solo recordings. Axel Stordahl was credited with the orchestral accompaniment on 'Night and Day' and 'The Night We Called It A Day', while Dorsey backed 'The Song Is You' and 'Lamplighter's Serenade'. Only after the session did Sinatra learn that, although bowing to popular pressure to let him go it alone, Dorsey had ensured that the discs were issued not on his own Victor label, but on that of the Bluebird subsidiary, a label that was treated in all respects as a lesser product. It was Dorsey's way of letting Sinatra have his way, hopefully to fall flat on his face.

But Sinatra already knew his way around the recording business. The relaxed, perfectionist recording artist of the later years was evident at that first session for Victor/Bluebird. Said Harry Meyerson, who had supervised the recording date, 'Frank was not like a band

vocalist at all. He came in self assured and slugging. He knew exactly what he wanted. He started out by having a good opinion of himself. On that first date, he stood his ground and displayed no humility, phoney or real.' But then, humility has never been a word much associated with Sinatra: knowing that he is great, he has never appeared to see any merit in hiding the fact.

Sinatra finally left Dorsey on 10 September, 1942. During the year, he had accompanied Dorsey once more to Hollywood, where the orchestra appeared in MGM's *Ship Ahoy*, which starred Red Skelton and Eleanor Powell, the latter using her tap-dancing skills to pass on messages in morse code! The Dorsey outfit were there for their music, nothing more, and Sinatra sang two songs, 'Poor You' and 'The Last Call For Love'. He even got a review mention, although not by name, in *The Hollywood Reporter*, whose critic wrote, 'The drummer and vocalist with Dorsey's orchestra have their moments.'

The last recording Sinatra made with Dorsey was in July 1942, 'There Are Such Things'. By December, it was Number One on the hit parade, and, by then, Sinatra was on his own. As Sinatra put it later: 'It was a very big gamble for me, leaving Tommy, but I figured that nobody had seriously challenged Bing Crosby since 1931. There were other guys coming up, and if they got the edge on me even by a few months, I might never have made it.'

If the clash of their egos had ensured that Sinatra and Dorsey would never have an easy relationship, Sinatra the musician learned an immense amount from Dorsey, a debt that has always been freely acknowledged: 'Tommy taught me every thing I knew about singing. He was my real education.' In particular, Sinatra learned breath control by watching Dorsey play. 'I discovered that "sneak-pinhole" in the

TWENTY CENTS   AUGUST 29, 1955

TIME

THE WEEKLY NEWSMAGAZINE

Donno Why I'm
Crazy Over Me—
The Hoboken Kid Acts

VOICES' N.Y. OPENER
NEEDS 142 COPS
in QUELL MOBS

Docks Columni
At Ciro's, Ch

Ava Stays Awa

Dramatic Roles
Lead Sinatra

FRANK SINATRA

$6.00 A YEAR   VOL. LXVI NO. 9

It Gets Lonely Early A pensive Sinatra during a recording session

inset **I've Got The World On A String** Sinatra makes the cover of *Time* in 1955, claiming: 'I'm going to do as I please. I don't need anybody. I did it all myself.'

corner of his mouth, not an actual pinhole but a tiny place where he was breathing. You know, in the middle of a phrase while the note was still flowing through the trombone, he'd take a quick breath and be able to play another four bars. Of course, it gave Tommy's playing a unique style and mellowness.' Sinatra's version of that 'pinhole' technique was to give his singing a unique style and mellowness too.

In addition to adapting Dorsey's technique and learning to breathe through his nose while singing, it has also been claimed by one of Sinatra's biographers that the singer entered on a programme of physical exercise designed to increase the capacity of his lungs with the result that he was able to inhale nearly half as much again as the 'ordinary' person. Whether or not Sinatra did in fact work out physically, one thing is certain: even at this relatively early stage in his career he had an impressive ability to use his voice to counterpoint his emerging mastery of the meaning and emotional shades behind the lyrics of his songs.

There was still nearly half his five-year contract with Dorsey left to run when the singer opted to leave, and Dorsey drove a hard bargain before allowing him his freedom. Sinatra had to sign a contract giving Dorsey and his business manager 43 per cent of his gross earnings for the next ten years. With him he took Henry (Hank) Sanicola, the one-time song plugger who had become mentor and friend and was to remain a business partner until their rift in the early Sixties, and Dorsey arranger Axel Stordahl. It was the end of Sinatra the band singer, and the beginning of Sinatra, the phenomenon.

♩ HOW LITTLE WE KNOW ♪

After over four decades as a professional entertainer, Frank Sinatra is still going strong, constantly adding to an already unassailable legend. His life and career are among the most fascinating in show-business history. Nevertheless, I have deliberately chosen to write in the greatest detail about his early years. Obviously, this approach is in no way intended to minimise the incredible events of the years that were to follow Sinatra's decision to become a solo artist, years that have made him the most successful and powerful entertainer in the world. Why, then, do the early years, already chronicled, seem so important to me?

The answer is simple. Without resorting to paperback psychology, we are all the products of our heritage, our upbringing, and our early environment. The poet William Wordsworth wrote, 'The child is father of the man', and while the words themselves have become a cliché, their inherent truth remains. Thus it seems to me that the key to Frank Sinatra's whole life and career lies in those boyhood years in Hoboken and the early days with Harry James and Tommy Dorsey. All the major traits and attitudes that have characterised his subsequent life and career were formed during those years: Sinatra the big spender and high liver; Sinatra the hard worker and perfectionist; Sinatra the fiery slugger, enemy of the media, and passionate defender of minority rights; Sinatra the unlikely but potent sex symbol, and Sinatra the unique stylist. Other persona had yet to emerge: Sinatra the actor, film director and producer of movies; Sinatra the businessman, entrepreneur and tycoon, and, finally, Sinatra the legend. But these were already within the man, dormant and awaiting only the right stimuli to bring them into effect.

Although only his subsequent life and career could demonstrate the fact, when Frank Sinatra left Tommy Dorsey his legendary status was already confirmed. The accumulated experience of his early years had seen to that.

Manhattan to Malindi

Sinatra's sense of timing was as impeccable in real life as it was on disc. The strike of recording musicians called by James Petrillo of the American Federation of Musicians in late 1942 turned out to be the beginning of the end for the Big Bands: the heavy overheads on touring meant that they had to rely on recordings for their continued existence. The era of the solo singer was at hand and Sinatra was ready to launch it.

While Dick Haymes took his place with the Dorsey Orchestra (and it is worth noting that, for all Dorsey's training and musicianship, only Sinatra made it really big of all his male singers), Sinatra himself went to Hollywood, to try for the job of staff singer on NBC. He failed to get it, instead singing Cole Porter's 'Night and Day' in Columbia's *Reveille With Beverly*, a three-minute appearance that had John T. McManus writing prophetically: '. . . it is reportable news that at each moan and trick-turn of the Sinatra voice, in fact each time he so much as turns his dead-pan head or flickers an eyelid, the adolescent set goes absolutely nuts! They squeal with delight; they rock and moan and make little animal cries. When he is finished, they are emotionally spent.' That was only on film. By the time *Reveille With Beverly* was released in 1943, Sinatra would be creating the same sexual havoc with live audiences—the Age of Swoon was at hand.

Once back in New York, Sinatra's career began to take off. Through Mannie Sachs of Columbia Records, he got a recording contract and his own CBS radio show, 'Songs by Sinatra'. He also got an introduction to General Amusement Corporation (GAC), who signed him to exclusive representation. Immediately he was booked into the less than prestigious Mosque Theater in Newark, New Jersey, where it was figured that a local boy could hardly fail to succeed. By the end of November 1942, his representative at GAC, Harry Romm, had managed to persuade Bob Weitman, managing director of the Paramount Theater in New York, to come and see the effect his young client was having on the kids in the audience. So impressed was Weitman with what he saw–he was later to state, 'I thought, you should excuse the expression, his pants had fallen down'–that he arranged for Sinatra to appear as an 'Extra Added Attraction' in the stage show due to open at the Paramount on the last day of December 1942, with the movie *Star-Spangled Rhythm*.

Although Sinatra's song 'There Are Such Things', which he had made with Dorsey, was high in the hit parade, the headliner at the Paramount, Benny Goodman, seemed unaware who 'that skinny kid' was. Recalled Peggy Lee, who was also on the bill, 'It was unbelievable. Benny gave him a pretty low-key introduction, I mean nothing *that* special. He said something like "And now, Frank Sinatra." And Frank walked out to the most deafening row you heard in your life.' In fact, as Sinatra described it: 'The sound that greeted me was absolutely deafening. It was a tremendous roar . . . I was scared stiff. I couldn't move a muscle. Benny froze too. He turned around and asked, "What the hell is that?" I burst out laughing and gave out with 'For Me and My Gal'.'

left Solo Sinatra, here with Axel Stordahl (on the stool) and pianist-actor-wit Oscar Levant (centre)

below For his song in 1943's *Reveille With Beverly*, Sinatra appears 'surrounded by adoring young women'

The literal answer to Goodman's question was that an almost tangible wall of sound had come from the auditorium and stopped him in his tracks. It was a genuinely unexpected occurrence, something brought about purely by the presence of the 'Extra Added Attraction'. Sinatra had not even begun to sing, he had merely been announced and had, as a result, created the wildest outbreak of mass female hysteria since the death of Rudolph Valentino. 'The Voice' had undoubtedly arrived, and an unassailable part of the Sinatra legend had been established.

In that one instant, Sinatra's mere presence had earned for him the epithet accorded him by *The New Yorker*, 'An American Phenomenon'.

You can't keep a good caption down! The one for this photograph read: 'The young Frank Sinatra who made the teenagers swoon . . .'

It was a phenomenon that owed everything to Sinatra himself and nothing to the kind of advertising and marketing techniques used today to promote new so-called 'stars'. With a single, well-documented appearance on the stage of the Paramount Theater, Sinatra *was* a star: all that was to follow during that first performance, and subsequent appearances, would only serve to emphasise the fact. As it was, the thunderous roar from the bobbysoxers was in no way calmed when Sinatra began to sing, softly and sweetly. Instead, the pandemonium was intensified. The girls screamed and shouted until they were hoarse, they moaned and writhed, they jumped up on their seats, they wet their pants and many chose to faint. The word 'swoon' was brought back into common usage once more.

The scenes of hysteria and bedlam continued for the eight weeks that Sinatra remained at the Paramount, exceeding anything ever before aroused by a performer. His fan mail rose to over one thousand letters weekly. The theatre had to engage extra guards to control the crowds, both inside and outside the theatre, and elaborate plans had to be put into action to smuggle Sinatra in and out. On those occasions when the fans managed to catch up with him, his clothes and belongings were ripped from him and once he was nearly strangled when two girls pulled either end of his bow tie. Little wonder that the Sinatra of later years was unable to stand being touched. His continuing effect on the bobbysoxers was neatly summed up by *Time* magazine, which wrote, 'Not since the days of Rudolph Valentino has American womanhood made such unabashed love to an entertainer.' Nor, it might have added, had the reverse been so obviously true.

Sinatra had learned more than just phrasing and technique when he listened as a teenager to Mabel Mercer, who, he later said, had taught him the way to use lyrics, and to Billie Holliday and Fats Waller. He had also learned how to include an extra ingredient in his songs, something that had been missing in the performances of previous leading male singers. That ingredient was sex. Sinatra had already demonstrated that he had a powerful attraction for women – the crowds at the stage doors on his tours with the James and Dorsey bands had proved that. Now he was infusing raw sex appeal into his singing, making love to each

Dubbed 'The Voice', Sinatra becomes 'An American Phenomenon', creating mass hysteria among the nation's bobbysoxers, and his fan mail is reputed to average between 2500 and 3000 letters a week. Fans are always on hand (*below*) to meet their idol and give him presents

moaning bobbysoxer in the audience. There were other explanations offered for his impact, of course: he was merely a by-product of wartime degeneracy, or the slight, lean and strangely vulnerable-looking singer was arousing the maternal instinct in his listeners, or any number of equally likely theories. What was certain was the effect itself and the fact that every woman in the audience felt that Sinatra was singing to her alone.

But Sinatra was to prove that his attraction was not limited to the bobbysoxers or the largely unsophisticated Paramount audience, often composed of children playing truant from school to catch up with their idol. Again being billed as 'Extra Added Attraction', to headliners comedian Walter O'Keefe and comedienne Sheila Barrett, Sinatra opened at the then failing Riobamba Club. His appearances there saved the club from bankruptcy and proved to Sinatra that his appeal was just as potent among older, richer, and more sophisticated women as it was with the bobby soxers.

Sinatra had arrived. He was the main topic of conversation among show-business people in

opposite Sinatra rehearses for his radio show 'Your Hit Parade' in 1943

left Appearing with the New York Philharmonic Orchestra, Sinatra is described as 'Plenty upstage and obnoxious at rehearsals', no doubt accounting for conductor Max Steiner's sour expression

below 'Lovely To Look At'

bottom From the London *Daily Mail*: 14 September, 1944

New York, the subject of club and vaudeville jokes. He achieved nationwide fame and coverage when, in February 1943, he took over the starring spot in the Lucky Strike cigarettes radio show, 'Your Hit Parade'. Networked across America on Saturday nights, the programme was the most popular on the air and it made Sinatra into a household name even more effectively than his records had done.

In mid May, he returned to the Paramount Theater, this time as undoubtedly the star attraction. His reception was, if anything, more hysterical and adulatory than on his previous stint. This time he was drawing $3,100 a week: six years before that, as waiter, master of ceremonies, and occasional singer at New Jersey's Rustic Cabin, his weekly pay had been $15. His influence was being felt abroad too.

Sinatra's Voice 'a Peril'

From Daily Mail Correspondent

MONTREAL, Wednesday. — Vancouver School Board have asked their music supervisor to report on the influence of Frank Sinatra, radio and screen crooner, on school children.

Some board members thought his singing demoralising, but one remarked: "Suppose we find Sinatra has a bad effect, what are we going to do? We cannot prevent them listening to him."

opposite A star is groomed. The original publicity caption claimed that Sinatra has 'his own personal secretary, Jerry O'Shea, who takes dictation, buffers his public, arranges appointments, answers fan mail, gets him here and there on the dot and protects him from his favorite vice–too many doughnuts!'

below right George Evans, Sinatra's skilled press agent, who helped minimise the public impact of his client's romances . . .

below left . . . including the one with Lana Turner, seen arriving for the 1943 Academy Awards ceremony with her husband, Stephen Crane, Sinatra, and Gloria de Haven

Having achieved stardom as a band singer, and a recording artist, as well as provoking the most stupendous audience reaction ever known in the theatre, Sinatra had only one more entertainment medium to make his own–the movies. He could afford to ignore his previous Hollywood appearances, the two films with the Dorsey band and his unbilled appearance in *Reveille With Beverly*. He signed to star in a movie for RKO.

♫ THE ONE I LOVE BELONGS TO SOMEBODY ELSE ♪

If Sinatra's career was clearly in the ascendant, his marriage was far from ideal. For a while, the couple managed to achieve a measure of closeness as Sinatra found himself having to come to terms with his sudden and uncontrollable effect on young women. This was something on a far larger scale than the crowds around the stage doors on band tours, where a casual intimacy could solve everything. Sinatra needed the emotional anchor that Nancy could provide while he searched within himself for the ability to cope.

Their new-found closeness was to be transient, but in the meantime, Sinatra bought them a new, six-roomed house in the quiet New Jersey town of Hasbrouck Heights, a place of peace and privacy, light years removed from the crowded and hostile streets of Hoboken. And then he left home on his way to Hollywood, leaving Nancy who was pregnant for the second time.

No-one fought harder for Sinatra than his then press agent, George Evans, who involved himself in garnering favourable publicity for his client's public and private life. Strangely, Sinatra's extra-marital affairs appeared only to reinforce his popular image with his fans. Yet Evans's task was a doubly difficult one since not only was he faced with trying to keep his client's name relatively scandal-free but he also became the go-between in an attempt to save Sinatra's marriage. Nancy was still in New Jersey while Sinatra was receiving – and enjoying – the full Hollywood star treatment. There was temptation everywhere, compounded by his own proven attractiveness to women. The story goes that while filming *Higher and Higher* Sinatra compiled a personal list of over twenty of Hollywood's most attractive female stars, put it up in his dressing-room at RKO, and ticked off each name as the conquest was made: legend has it that by the time the movie was completed, so was the list.

Certainly, Sinatra's romance with Lana Turner was public enough, despite such ruses as Evans going along with the couple, pretending to be Turner's date. But, by the time of Sinatra's first separation from Nancy in 1946, Turner was announcing to gossip columnist Louella Parsons, 'I am not in love with Frank and he is not in love with me. I have never in my life broken up a home. I just can't take these accusations.' Cynics held that Turner had been romancing Sinatra as a means of attracting the attention – and the jealousy – of millionaire Howard Hughes.

Sinatra had more in common with Marilyn Maxwell than the worldly Lana Turner, who epitomised the so-called 'sophistication' of Hollywood. Maxwell, like Sinatra, was a newcomer to Hollywood and was finding the adjustment to the new environment a difficult one. She had also been a band singer, with Buddy Rogers and Ted Weems, before embarking on a screen career. Here too, George Evans had to go into action in order to keep their romance out of the headlines as much as possible and he is generally credited with finally severing the relationship.

Sinatra was now represented by the Music Corporation of America (MCA), the largest talent agency there was. They had wheeled and dealed to set him free from his financial and contractual entanglements, not least of which was the iniquitous contract he had been forced to sign to break away from Tommy Dorsey. Now Sinatra owned enough of himself to be able to reap the benefit of his immense earning power.

The 'official' version of the severance of his contract with Dorsey is that it cost MCA $35,000, plus a separate agreement they entered into with GAC, Sinatra's previous agent. In addition, out of advance royalties from Colum-

bia Records, Sinatra himself had to pay $25,000. There can be no doubt that Sinatra bitterly resented paying so much of what he earned to the bandleader and that he was determined to end the contract. Shortly before it was terminated, he told the media, 'You can quote Sinatra as saying that he believes it is wrong for anybody to own a piece of him and collect on it when the owner is doing nothing for Sinatra.'

There is another, mythical, version of the ending of the contract. It arose out of allegations that have been made throughout Sinatra's career about his supposed links with the Mafia. That these unproven allegations should have been made in the first place is not altogether surprising. Sinatra is of Italian-American origin and he grew up in an Italian area of New Jersey that was dominated by Mafia mobsters; such allegations would inevitably have applied to anyone growing up in the same place at the same time. Thus, the legend grew that Willie Moretti, a Mafia don from the part of New Jersey in which Sinatra had grown up, had personally intervened with Dorsey over the matter of the contract, pushed a gun into the bandleader's mouth, and 'persuaded' him to 'sell' Sinatra's contract: the reputed price – one dollar. This was pure fiction, as was pointed out by Earl Wilson in his recent biography, *Sinatra*, quoting a source he believes to be reliable as saying: 'It couldn't be true. Frank was just a kid. He didn't know people like that. . . .'

Nevertheless, wilder and wilder allegations about his so-called Mafia connections were to become as much a part of Sinatra's life as his battles with the media and his reputation as a ladies man. For instance, in a story that manages to combine both Mafia and women, it is claimed that in the files of the Justice Department is a telegram sent to Sinatra by Moretti in 1950 at the height of the scandal of his public 'courtship' of Ava Gardner and the break-up of his marriage to Nancy. Signing himself 'Willie Moore' – apparently a well-known alias of his – Moretti played the moralist, cabling, 'I am very much surprised what I have been reading in the newspapers between you and your darling wife. Remember you have a decent wife and children. You should be very happy. Regards to all. Willie Moore.'

Back in 1943, Sinatra's movie career began with all the omens looking good. There was his

left Sinatra and co-star Michele Morgan in a scene from *Higher and Higher*

below Hello sailor! MGM were quick to capitalise on their new contract star's fame as this off-set still from *Anchors Aweigh* shows

left In a carefully staged 'candid' shot, RKO's publicists found Sinatra and co-star Gloria de Haven 'asleep' on the set of *Step Lively*

arrival in Hollywood itself, an event that turned out to be impressive even by that town's standards of ballyhoo. It had been planned that Sinatra would leave the *Santa Fe Chief* at Pasadena in order to avoid the waiting teenagers at Los Angeles Station. To the surprise of no-one except the incorrigibly naive, Sinatra was surrounded and mobbed at Pasadena by some five to six thousand screaming bobby-soxers. That evening, 14 August, Sinatra appeared to sing at the Hollywood Bowl with the famous Hollywood Bowl Symphony Orchestra, the last of four famous orchestras with whom Sinatra had been singing on his way to Hollywood, another neat publicity stunt devised by the resourceful George Evans. The Hollywood Bowl concert was a sell-out. The Sinatra magic worked as well as it had done in New York and he was mobbed again as he left after the concert.

Sinatra stayed in Hollywood for two months, making his RKO film, *Higher and Higher*, a title that promised well for his film career and which was to hold true – for a while. The making of the film came easily to Sinatra, who took to acting, finding it less of an effort to master than music. One thing he did object to was the constant need for takes and re-takes, feeling that he always gave of his best on the first take, before staleness set in. As his muscle as a movie actor increased, he would become famous for his 'one take' method of movie-making. *Higher and Higher* gave him five songs, written for him by Jimmy McHugh and Harold Adamson and arranged by Axel Stordahl. One of them, 'I Couldn't Sleep a Wink Last Night', became an Oscar nominee for 1944. Despite being billed as a co-star, after nominal stars Michèle Morgan and Jack Haley, RKO publicised the movie as 'The Sinatra Show', a move that paid off at the box-office, if not particularly with the critics.

During his time at RKO, Sinatra was re-united with Harry James, then playing at the Hollywood Canteen. They performed 'All Or Nothing At All', the song, according to Sinatra in an interview with Louella Parsons, which

opposite A Star at War! Sinatra as he appeared in a US Treasury Department propaganda movie, 1945's *The All-Star Bond Rally*

below Sinatra was often faced by heckling servicemen on his overseas USO tours because he didn't make the grade for military service

right Sing to Win: V-discs were issued by the US Government for US Army and Navy personnel. Some, such as 124B, were specially recorded; others were commercial pressings

had got them thrown out of Victor Hugo's not that many years before. To his surprise, in his free time, Sinatra found himself missing Nancy, despite the obvious romantic possibilities in Hollywood and mentioned her whenever he gave interviews, and on the Bing Crosby radio show.

When he returned to New Jersey after completing the movie, his immediate concern was his draft status, and his fans took it badly when in October he was declared 1-A. He left his New Jersey home and Nancy in December to report to Newark for his pre-induction medical. To his immense personal chagrin, and to the accompaniment of highly vocal jubilation, tears, and cheers from the fans who had followed him to Newark, Sinatra was rejected for military service. His left eardrum was punctured. He had genuinely wanted to serve his country: instead, he had to make do with USO (United Service Organisation) tours, performing for servicemen in America and, later, overseas both in Europe and Africa.

♪ AS LONG AS THERE'S MUSIC ♪

When he returned to Hollywood for his second RKO film, *Step Lively*, Sinatra *knew* he was a star and a sex symbol for a complete generation. He also knew that he could not allow himself to be drained of his energies, as he had while making *Higher and Higher*. The studio system that so often left him at the mercy of press agents and his director, the (as he saw it) unnecessary rehearsals and re-takes, all began to bring out the other Sinatra, the man of temper and temperament, liable to lash out violently at relatively minor provocations. He also began to react to the reality of stardom as he learned that a star has no life that is not considered newsworthy and therefore fit to be shared with a world eager for insight, information, and mere gossip. While making this second film, Sinatra came fully to understand—and use to his advantage—the power that was the obverse side to the lack of privacy afforded a star. When he wanted it, *Step Lively* was filmed *his* way, or he simply held things up until it was. It was a simple technique and, given the economics of movie-making and the growing power of Sinatra, it almost always worked.

One feature of Sinatra's life and career has received more coverage and publicity than almost any other, most of it totally disproportionate to the events themselves. This is, of course, his relationship with the media. It is a relationship that has often been stormy, rancorous, and acrimonious, frequently erupting into verbal and physical violence on both sides. There have been the legendary personal feuds with people now totally forgotten except in the context of their battles with Sinatra, and there has been a constant accretion of gossip and innuendo, unproven links with organised crime, and all the other stories which make up the largely mythical public Sinatra, the man who has been seen almost always in conflict with the Fourth Estate.

> **'S**inatra's idea of paradise is a place where there are plenty of women and no newspapermen. He doesn't know it, but he'd be better off if it were the other way round.'
> HUMPHREY BOGART

This is largely due to the fact that, like all public figures, anything Sinatra has done as a private individual has been seen by the media as legitimate source material for publicity, comment, distortion, and often downright invention. One of the most consistent character traits displayed by Sinatra has been his often near obsessive determination to keep his public and private personae as far apart as possible, and this, given the inevitable role of the media in society, has been the cause of much of the well-documented friction and hostility. It is an aspect of Sinatra which has been so

'Sinatra felled me with a single blow'

HOLLYWOOD, Wednesday.
—"Frank Sinatra felled me with a single blo— New York colum— told "

Sinatra's explosive night out

From ROLAND ATKINSON, Paris, Tuesday

SINGING star Frank Sinatra started a near-riot here tonight. Angered by photographers while going "on the town." he pulled some thunderflashes from his pocket and threw them at cameramen outside his hotel.

exhaustively—and exhaustingly—covered and re-covered, mostly by the media themselves, often in an incestuous or cannibalistic way, that it is unnecessary to go over that well-trodden ground once more, except tangentially. The continuing war between Sinatra and the press, radio, and television is documented elsewhere.

Much of the friction between Sinatra and the media has been due to the fact that Sinatra, unlike other, more ephemeral entertainers, is clearly *not* a creation of the media but the product of his own talent and abilities. That talent has enabled him to communicate directly with his public, and the media have been reduced to a role in which they appear to give greater emphasis to the man than the artist. It is tempting, therefore, to believe that Sinatra would whole-heartedly subscribe to what W. C. Fields was quoted as saying of those who criticised him, 'Tomorrow, thousands of the non-tissue using public will be using this for

you-know-what.' Indeed, Sinatra has it on record that he uses newspapers to line the bottom of his parrot's cage or as a training aid for his dog.

Certain events of 1944 are worth chronicling briefly here since they indicate the genesis of Sinatra's friction with the media. The key to that mutual hostility is here.

On 10 January, 1944, on the set of *Step Lively*, Sinatra was told that he had become a father for the second time. He named the boy Franklin Wayne, in admiration of Democratic president Franklin D. Roosevelt. Later that year, Sinatra went to Washington with restauranteur Toots Shor and comedian Rags Ragland and, at a reception at the White House, met President Roosevelt. Roosevelt was reported as telling him, 'Fainting, which was so prevalent, has become a lost art among the ladies. I'm glad you have revived it.'

Sinatra, who had learned politics as a child from his mother, joined the campaign to re-elect

Roosevelt to a fourth term of office. This marked his emergence as a political figure, Sinatra claiming that he was campaigning as an individual and not as an entertainer. Inevitably, however, when he spoke on radio and at rallies, it was his impact as a singer that added power to his endorsement. It also drew upon him the animus of the press opposed to Roosevelt, in particular the Hearst newspaper chain, who were implacable in their hatred of the New Deal.

His experiences under attack by the media soured for ever Sinatra's relationship with them and he articulated his bitterness later. 'My first real criticism from the press came when I campaigned for President Roosevelt in 1944. A few columnists took me to task, insisting that entertainers should stick to entertaining. Most stars agree with this. They also realise it is bad public relations to indulge in politics because you may lose fans who don't agree with you. However, I feel it is the duty of every American citizen to help elect the candidate of his choice. Ginger Rogers, George Murphy and other stars supported Tom Dewey during the campaign *and I noted that none of my critics lambasted them.*' Despite later attempts at reconciliation, the best that the future would provide was an uneasy truce, broken by occasional bitter fighting. Attitudes had been formed and had hardened.

Sinatra's third appearance at the Paramount Theater, New York, led to the legendary Columbus Day riots, proving that his political involvement had in no way damaged his appeal. On the first day of the engagement, Sinatra had to enter the theatre at 6.00 a.m. Some of the bobbysoxers had been queuing since the previous afternoon and there were already a thousand hopefuls in line. The next day, however, was Columbus Day, 12 October and a school holiday. The theatre was besieged, the box-office destroyed: despite the drafting of extra police, there was no way in which the unprecedented crowd could be controlled. Police estimates put a figure of some ten thousand lining up to get into a theatre that held only 3,500, while a further twenty thousand surrounded the Paramount, flooded into Times Square, and brought traffic to a complete standstill. It was a unique event, never to be repeated, except by carefully orchestrated and planned 'demonstrations' for future entertainment phenomena such as the Beatles.

♪WE HATE TO LEAVE♫

The Columbus Day riots also marked a watershed in Sinatra's career. It was the peak of his period as teenage idol and the beginning of the cooling off of his love affair with the bobbysoxers. With the war ending, the soldiers for whom Sinatra had been a surrogate figure were coming home. But as the teenage idol and 'The Voice' faded, the new Sinatra began to emerge: this was Sinatra the movie star and major singer. And it was not only the audiences that were changing. Sinatra, too, was undergoing a metamorphosis, brought about by his sudden rise to stardom, his newly acquired wealth, and by the power and influence they conferred upon him. It was a change that was ultimately to lead to the break-up of his marriage.

Realising that his future was likely to lie in Hollywood and wanting to see more of his family, Sinatra bought Mary Astor's old house in the San Fernando Valley. In mid 1944, he brought Nancy and the two children from New Jersey to what Nancy was to dub 'the house that music built'. However, despite Sinatra's efforts—including the gift of a diamond watch on their first evening in the new house, and a Cadillac and driving lessons—it became clear that Nancy was finding the transition from New

Nice Work If You Can Get It In *Four For Texas* (Sam Company 1964), the four are Ursula Andress, Dean Martin, Sinatra, and Anita Ekberg

Jersey housewife to the wife of a Hollywood star a difficult one to make. Sinatra had largely 'gone Hollywood': she could not, or would not, do the same. Again, Sinatra was surrounded by one of the all-male groups of friends and hangers-on that were to become a characteristic part of his life style. Nancy did not like this group–which included Hank Sanicola, song writers Sammy Cahn and Jule Styne, and Sinatra's arranger and conductor Axel Stordahl–and she did not hide her dislike. Sinatra began to spend less time at home. At the same time, in a town as open and prone to gossip as Hollywood, Nancy could not fail to be aware of Sinatra's growing reputation as a ladies' man, despite all the efforts of his press agent, George Evans.

The musicians' union strike had brought the death of the Big Bands and had also caused a temporary hiatus in Sinatra's career as a recording artist. He indulged in a brief, strike-avoiding flurry of *a capella* (vocal backing) recordings in 1943, the same year that saw the re-release of his 1939 recording with the Harry James band of 'All Or Nothing At All', a disc that made the top of the hit parade. Finally, in autumn 1944, Columbia Records settled with the musicians' union and Sinatra's recording career started again. By the end of the year, under the guidance of Columbia's Mannie Sachs and with arranger-conductor Axel Stordahl, he had recorded seventeen songs. They tended to be songs from shows and movies and ones which allowed him to demonstrate his unique ability in phrasing lyrics. He was soon back in the hit parade.

Step Lively was released in 1944 while Sinatra was abroad entertaining American troops on a USO tour and its success led RKO to sign him to a seven-year contract. But Louis B. Mayer, encouraged by the success of *Step Lively* and the fact that *Metronome*'s poll made Sinatra the

Best Male Singer for the fourth straight year, decided that Sinatra would be an ideal addition to the MGM roster of stars.

When Mayer bought Sinatra's contract from RKO, Sinatra reputedly received $1,500,000 over seven years. In *Anchors Aweigh*, his first movie for MGM, he scored a considerable personal success, not just as a singer but also as an actor, thanks to careful casting, which had him playing a shy and love-sick sailor on shore leave, and the fact that star Gene Kelly carried the main burden of work. Two songs by Sinatra, 'I Fall in Love Too Easily' and 'The Charm of You', added to his impact, and the movie's general lightheartedness, inventive choreography, and the full glossy MGM treatment ensured its success. Said *Motion Picture Herald*, 'All the world knows Frank Sinatra can sing; now it turns out he can act too. His characterisation of Kelly's shipmate is delightful.' The making of the film in 1944 (*Anchors Aweigh* was released in 1945) had been marred by another Sinatra versus-the-press incident in which a United Press reporter covering location filming at the Hollywood Bowl quoted Sinatra as saying, 'Pictures stink. Most of the people in them do too.' The resulting furore, with its claims of misrepresentation, did nothing to improve Sinatra's liking of the media, or the longeurs of Hollywood film-making.

But also released in 1945 was the short (ten minute) film *The House I Live In*, made by Sinatra at RKO with director Mervyn LeRoy, a powerful indictment of racial intolerance and a plea for greater understanding. Sinatra, LeRoy, and writer Albert Maltz all contributed their services for nothing and the film won a special Oscar. This was another, lesser-known side of the Sinatra personality on view, the deeply committed battler for minority rights.

1945 seemed a first-rate year for Sinatra. As a recording artist, he cut some thirty-eight sides

with Mannie Sachs at Columbia, most of them ballads, the song form that was still popular, including 'If I Loved You' and 'Day by Day', the record that allegedly caused band singer Doris Kapelhoff to change her name to Doris Day. He also took time off to make the album *Frank Sinatra Conducts Alec Wilder*, no mean feat since he was unable to read music. Commented Wilder, 'What was so good about it was that it was so musical. Frank felt music and he listened carefully to the soloists and he built up a wonderful rapport with them and the other musicians.' He confirmed his talent with live audiences, winning the Act of the Year Award from *Metronome* after his appearance at New York's Waldorf Hotel. He also played the Paramount again and, while there were no street demonstrations outside the building, his effect on the audiences was still as orgasmically hysterical as ever it had been before.

♪ IT'S NICE TO GO TRAV'LIN ♪

In 1946, his records continued to sell well, particularly 'The Coffee Song' and the Sammy Cahn and Jule Styne number 'Five Minutes More'. But the first signs of strain had begun to appear as Sinatra embarked on a year in which he set himself too gruelling a work schedule, as well as continuing to enjoy a hectic night life. During 1946 he cut fifty-one songs in a total of fifteen sessions, as well as fulfilling a crowded schedule of radio work, theatre performances, and movies. He smashed records at theatres everywhere, but it was a tour that involved forty-five shows a week and it was obvious that Sinatra was overtaxing himself. By the end of the year his self-imposed strain was beginning to show up in his voice. More dramatically, it affected his marriage. On 7 October, it was announced that Sinatra and Nancy had parted.

It was hardly a surprise; the singer had seen little of his wife and children during his hectic working life, and his private life and liaisons were all too common knowledge in Hollywood.

During the separation, at a party at a Palm Springs nightclub, Sinatra danced with a woman who had come as the companion of millionaire Howard Hughes. Her name was Ava Gardner. But, due to the efforts of his friends, Sinatra and Nancy were reconciled, in the full glare of the spotlight during a performance at a night spot by comedian Phil Silvers. Nancy accompanied him to New York for his date at the Waldorf and Sinatra announced at a press conference that they were completely reconciled and that he and Nancy would spend more time together.

The year had begun with Sinatra being named by *Down Beat* as Favourite Male Singer for the third successive year. It ended with *Metronome* readers choosing him Best Singer of the Year. He had also been voted Most Popular Screen Star of the Year by the readers of *Modern Screen*, beating Cornel Wilde and Van Johnson. But in Hollywood itself, after a year characterised by his feuds with his studio, the Screen Actors Guild, and, especially, the media, Sinatra earned the epithet Least Cooperative Star of 1946 from the Hollywood Women's Press

opposite Family matters: Sinatra and first wife Nancy after six years of marriage

above Sinatra poses for a publicity still, 'hearing' the news of his son's birth in November 1944, while the proud father was making *Step Lively*

left Nancy Sr and Nancy Jr meet up with Walter Pidgeon at MGM's studios

'Ration what they like, but ration Frankie Sinatra and they'll have ME to reckon with.'

Club, an important publicity outlet.

About the best thing that happened to Sinatra in 1947 was the celebration of Frank Sinatra Day in Hoboken on 13 October. Otherwise, the year was marked by a dramatic deterioration in his relationship with the media.

Professionally, he was under attack in Hollywood by Louella Parsons, one of the then reigning gossip columnists (the other was the equally repellent, failed-actress Hedda Hopper) whose disproportionate power through their newspaper syndication and radio shows amounted on many occasions to something nearer blackmail than journalism. Hated and feared as

she was by her 'subjects', Parsons was a major force to be contended with and the feud that developed between her and Sinatra only served to exacerbate his already strained relations with MGM. She printed in *Modern Screen* a telegram which she had received from Sinatra which read in part: 'I'll begin by saying that if you care to make a bet, I'll be glad to take your money that MGM and Frank Sinatra do not part company, permanently or othewise. Secondly, Frankie has not been a very difficult boy on the lot ... Last, but not least, in the future I'll appreciate your not wasting your breath in any lectures because when I feel I need one I'll seek such advice from someone who

either writes or tells the truth. . . .' The feud continued with Parsons offering the olive branch but still printing such remarks as 'He isn't a well boy, and when I heard he was really ill, he had my deepest sympathy. I was ill for a long, long time last year myself and I know that when you are sick, you just aren't yourself. What I am trying to say is that I can understand Frank's short temper and the way he feels. . . .' If there was anything more repellent than castigation from Parsons, it was sympathy.

Much more serious than the damage that lady was able to inflict on his movie career was the slew of newspaper stories that attempted to tie Sinatra firmly in with the Mafia and with mob leader Lucky Luciano, one-time top Mafia gangster who had finally been put in jail in 1936 by New York prosecutor Thomas E. Dewey. Luciano served only ten years of a sentence that had been for a minimum of thirty years, being paroled in 1946 for what was claimed to be his help in facilitating the Allies' landings in Sicily during World War Two. The man who pardoned him was none other than Thomas E. Dewey, now Governor of New York. A condition of Luciano's parole was that he would be deported to his native Italy, but an apparently under-cover agreement was made to allow him to return to his crime syndicate activities in the United States.

By the beginning of 1947, Luciano was in Havana, Cuba, making preparations for his comeback. Robert Ruark, then a reporter and columnist for the Scripps-Howard newspaper chain, saw Luciano holding court at the Hotel Nacional, where he had become something of a tourist attraction. Ruark wrote a series of columns from Havana towards the end of February, with the object of attacking Luciano, who was then being visited by the top American mobsters before his return to the United States.

====

'I think Frank has always had a secret desire to be a hoodlum. But he's got too much class, too much sense, to permit him to go that route.'

BING CROSBY

====

And in Ruark's columns came the first and most damaging 'exposés' of Sinatra's alleged links with the Mafia. These stories, picked up and embroidered by other journalists and radio

commentators, formed the basis for most sub-sequent items about Sinatra's apparent associa-tion with organised crime.

Ruark's target was undoubtedly Luciano but, in the process of his onslaught, Sinatra was badly hit for a visit he made to Cuba in 1947. Wrote Ruark in his column on 20 February, 'Sinatra was here for four days last week and during that time his companion in public and in private was Luciano, Luciano's bodyguards and a rich collection of gamblers and high-binders. The friendship was beautiful. They were seen together at the race track, the gambling casino and at special parties. In addition to Mr Luciano, I am told that Ralph Capone was present . . . and so was a rather large and well-matched assortment of the goons who find the south salubrious in the winter, or grand jury time. But Mr Sinatra, the self-confessed saviour of the country's small fry, seems to be setting a most peculiar example for his hordes of pimply, shrieking slaves.' This, added to a headline which read 'SHAME, SINATRA!' and references to the Mafia chief as 'Sinatra's buddy' and 'Sinatra's boyfriend', brought Sinatra under concerted attack from huge sections of the media, in particular those areas of the right-wing press opposed to his liberal views and his stance on race relations. One of the most virulent of these attackers was a long-time Sinatraphobe, Lee Mortimer, columnist of the New York *Mirror*.

♪ THE SKY FELL DOWN ♪

Sinatra was reported as having flown from Miami to Havana with Rocco and Joseph Fischetti, who were reputedly associated with Mob activities. Much later, in 1951, Lee Mortimer claimed in the New York *Mirror* that the purpose of Sinatra's visit to Havana had been to deliver $2,000,000 in small bills to Luciano. This was a charge rapidly and effec-tively refuted by Sinatra who responded, 'Picture me, skinny Frankie, lifting $2,000,000 in small bills. For the record, $1,000 in dollar bills weighs three pounds, which makes the load I am supposed to have carried six thousand pounds. Even assuming that the bills were $20s, the bag would still have required a couple of stevedores to carry it. This is probably the most ridiculous charge that has ever been levelled at me . . . I stepped off the plane in Havana with a

left The bust things in life are free! Commissioned by *Modern Screen* magazine, sculptor Jo Davidson goes about recreating a solid Sinatra

below Local boy makes good. Sinatra, flanked by his parents, helps celebrate Frank Sinatra Day in Hoboken on 30 October, 1947

small bag in which I carried my oils, sketching material and personal jewelry, which I never send with my regular luggage.'

But in 1947, at the height of the furore, Sinatra was quoted as saying, 'I was brought up to shake a man's hand when I am introduced to him without first investigating his past. Any report that I fraternised with goons or racketeers is a vicious lie.'

It was some five years later, in *American*

Weekly, that Sinatra got around to offering a full explanation to the obvious charge that he, along with millions of other Americans, would have needed no background investigations to recognise some of the more notorious and well-publicised gangsters. His explanation: 'What actually happened is that in 1947 I had some time off and decided to vacation in Havana and Mexico City. On the way, I stopped off at Miami to play a benefit for the Damon Runyon Cancer

opposite Song-and-dance men. Sinatra as Dennis Ryan and Gene Kelly as Eddie O'Brien in a vaudeville routine from the 1949 movie *Take Me Out To The Ball Game*

above left Sinatra rehearses a song from *It Happened In Brooklyn* with composer Jule Styne at the piano, lyricist Sammy Cahn standing, and director Richard Whorf looking on

below left Frank Jr and Nancy Jr visit their father, Gene Kelly, and Esther Williams on the set of *Take Me Out To The Ball Game*

Fund. I ran into Joe Fischetti there and when he found I was headed for Havana, he told me he and his brothers were going too. He changed his reservations to be on my plane . . .

'That night, I was having a drink at the bar with Connie Immerman, a New York restaurateur, and met a large group of men and women. As so often happens in big groups, the introductions were perfunctory. I was invited to have dinner with them and while dining, I realised that one of the men in the party was Lucky Luciano. It suddenly struck me that I was leaving myself open to criticism by remaining at the table, but I could think of no way to leave in the middle of dinner without creating a scene.

'After dinner I went to the jai alai games and then, with an acquaintance, toured the night spots. We finally wound up at the Havana Casino where we passed a table at which were Luciano and several other men. They insisted that we sit down for a drink. Again, rather than cause a disturbance, I had a quick drink and excused myself. These were the only times I've ever seen Luciano in my life.'

However, Tony Scaduto in his book *Frank Sinatra* quotes a report from the Federal Narcotic Bureau that Sinatra spent four days with Luciano and his friends, as Ruark had claimed in his articles. And in 1962, when Italian police searched the Naples apartment in which Luciano had just died of a heart attack, they found a gold cigarette case with the inscription 'TO CHARLIE, FROM HIS PAL FRANK SINATRA'.

The same year, 1962, saw Bobby Kennedy, then Attorney General, use his position and Sinatra's alleged Mafia associations to persuade his brother, President John F. Kennedy, to break with Sinatra, in public, at least. Among the many inquiries instigated by Bobby Kennedy in his determined attack on Sinatra was one designed to elucidate whether Sinatra had cast Phyllis McGuire into his movie *Come*

below Sinatra arrives in Paris en route from visiting Ava Gardner in Spain

bottom Democratic days: Sinatra sits next to Eleanor Roosevelt at a studio function, with studio boss Dore Schary on her right. Melvyn Douglas converses with Mrs Roosevelt while Danny Kaye just looks bewildered

opposite Happy Days Are Here Again: Sinatra and Ava

Blow Your Horn because she was the girlfriend of Sam Giancana, a noted Mafia mobster.

Later, even more bizarre and convoluted relationships were to be revealed as the details of President Kennedy's womanising became public in the Seventies. Among his women friends had been one Judith Campbell Exner, once a friend of Sinatra's before he had introduced her to both Sam Giancana and John F. Kennedy. When Ms Judith Campbell Exner claimed at a press conference that she stopped having sexual relationships with Sinatra because of his allegedly 'kinky' tastes, Sinatra came back with a splendid riposte that deserves (and probably will receive) immortality. 'Hell,' said Sinatra, 'hath no fury like a hustler with a literary agent!'

However, back in 1947, when the Ruark-inspired furore was at its height, Sinatra finally settled some of his accounts physically, as was probably inevitable given the pressures he was under at the time and his own explosive temperament. He was constantly being baited by columnist Lee Mortimer over the Havana incidents and finally, in April 1947, Sinatra and Mortimer met up in Ciro's restaurant in Hollywood. Although the exact details of their encounter have never fully been established, the evening ended with Mortimer lying on the floor, the recipient of a hard punch from Sinatra. What has been established for certain is that the following day Sinatra was arrested while he was at a radio station and taken to Beverly Hills District Court. He pleaded 'not guilty' to a charge of battery and assault and, as he didn't have the necessary cash on him, friends in the courtroom helped raise his $500 bail. Sinatra wanted to fight the case but studio boss Louis B. Mayer insisted that he settle out of court: he did not want MGM associated with the obvious adverse publicity. Against his natural inclination to make a fight of it, Sinatra complied and paid the columnist an estimated $9,000.

His problems increased when he was accused, without any evidence being offered or any further action taken, of having left-wing leanings by the then rampant House Un-American Activities Committee, who were busy 'investigating' what they believed to be Communist infiltration of the movie industry. The result, for Sinatra, was further unfavourable publicity and a concomitant drop in his popularity, serving to confirm his fading star status.

This year of 1947 also marked a new direction in popular music trends, away from the crooner and balladeer exemplified by Sinatra and towards a tougher, more driving style of singing which began to absorb influences from Country and Western music. Singers in this new style, like Frankie Laine and Tony Bennett, helped reduce Sinatra's fans still further. Despite these signs of change, Sinatra made 1947 one of his most prolific years in the recording studios, cutting over sixty-eight sides in some twenty-five sessions. The sum total of this activity probably resulted in Sinatra suffering over-exposure.

Towards the end of the year, he returned to radio and the hit parade, this time with Doris Day. It did not help his career decline. Nor did his appearance at New York's Capitol Theater at the end of the year. Although the reviews were generally good, the audience reaction was not what was expected. There were no Paramount-style swooning scenes and generally attendances were poor. Whether as a result of the hammering he had taken in the media during the year, or the change in public taste, or a combination of both, the Capitol engagement failed dismally to reach the expected box-office takings.

The two films released in 1947 were *It Happened in Brooklyn* and the Jerome Kern biopic, *Till The Clouds Roll By*. The former was a pleasant enough, if minor, musical with a score by Sammy Cahn and Jule Styne and it did good business at the box-office, as well as gaining a generally favourable press for Sinatra and his co-stars Kathryn Grayson, Jimmy Durante, and Peter Lawford. *Newsweek* probably summed up the concensus when it wrote, '. . . Sinatra becomes a smoother performer every time out.' There was little that could be said in favour of his contribution to the lumpish *Till The Clouds Roll By*. He appeared in the finale, perched on top of what appeared to be a column made of pink candy, wearing a pink suit and singing 'Ol' Man River'. At best, it was a highly embarrassing moment: at worst it was what *Life* magazine said of it, selecting the scene as 'the worst single moment' of any film of that year.

1948 failed to stem Sinatra's professional decline. Not happy with Mayer's choice of scripts at MGM, he fought to be allowed to go back to RKO on loan to play a priest in *Miracle of the Bells*. Perhaps he hoped the role would do for him what priesthood had achieved for Bing Crosby in *Going My Way* (1944). In the event, *Miracle of the Bells* signally failed to revive his acting career and his portrayal of the priest did nothing to improve his public image. The film received a largely hostile press, which Sinatra took personally, and his ego took a terrible hammering. Things were made worse by the release of his next movie, MGM's *The Kissing Bandit*, generally regarded as the nadir of his film career. Even the fact that Sinatra received over $325,000 from films in 1948 did nothing to console him for these critical brickbats, and 1949's *Take Me Out To The Ball Game*, while a pleasant enough musical with Gene Kelly, Jules Munshin, Esther Williams, and Betty Garrett, put Sinatra in the role of a singing-and-dancing baseball player, which did nothing to stem his decline in the cinema.

This decline was being paralleled by Sinatra's continuing fall in popularity as a singer. Part of it was due to changes in taste, and to the fact that the bobbysoxers were growing up, but more and more it became clear that Sinatra was being supplanted by the newer singers who were establishing themselves. The sales of Sinatra's records fell throughout 1948 and 1949 and, at the end of 1949, came positive proof that Sinatra was on the way out as a singer. In the annual poll of male singers conducted by *Down Beat*, the Number One spot which Sinatra had filled for a number of years was now held by Billy Eckstine. Next came Frankie Laine, while Bing Crosby and Mel Torme shared third place. Sinatra came fifth. Only on radio, with two regular shows, did Sinatra's career look anything like healthy.

Time described Sinatra's last film for MGM, *On The Town* (1949), as: 'So exuberant that it threatens at moments to bounce right off the screen.' Its witty script, immense zest, musical score, and inventive choreography, as well as its then unusual use of New York locations, all combined to turn the film into a classic musical. It was a critical success and a box-office hit, both of more value to MGM than Sinatra.

Sinatra, however, could have had few illusions that it was his presence in the film that made it a success. As had been the case with *Anchors Aweigh*, he was once again playing second fiddle to star Gene Kelly, who not only took up most of the burden in front of the camera but also co-directed the film with Stanley Donen. Sinatra was very much in Kelly's shadow and the role itself was little more than a reprise of his part in *Anchors Aweigh*: once more he was playing a shy sailor on furlough, the difference being that this time shore leave was in New York and not Los Angeles. For Sinatra, who wanted to become a serious actor–hence his fight to make *Miracle of the Bells* against the wishes of MGM–*On The Town* merely re-confirmed his position as a musical-comedy star. In any case, when he came to New York in December 1949 for the premiere of *On The Town* at Radio City Music Hall, he was once more to meet Ava Gardner. Their subsequent courtship finally destroyed both his

left Art imitates Life: Sinatra in a scene with Alex Nicol from *Meet Danny Wilson*

below Nancy testifies in a Santa Monica Court in September 1950, winning custody of the children and separate maintenance. She makes no mention of Sinatra's flagrant romance with Ava Gardner, citing instead mental cruelty

opposite By January 1952, when they attended the Hollywood premiere of Ava's movie *Pandora and The Flying Dutchman*, she and Sinatra had been married for just over a month

disintegrating marriage and the remnants of his career.

♪CHANGE PARTNERS ♪

By that December, his marriage was all but over, despite the birth of the Sinatras' third child, Christina, in Hollywood's Cedars of Lebanon Hospital on 20 July, 1948. As his career declined and his public image became progressively less attractive, Sinatra, despite reconciliations and sporadic attempts to play the role of family man, had found himself increasingly less inclined to attempt to patch up the marriage. The assaults on his ego from all sides and the unpalatable fact that his career appeared to be rapidly coming to an inglorious end put him under far too much pressure merely to survive. His public reconciliation with Nancy in 1946 was forgotten, as was the promise to build them a house in Connecticut. Instead, he paid $250,000 for a mansion in the Holmby Hills area of Beverly Hills, near the home of Humphrey Bogart, and moved Nancy and their children into it, while he continued in his own way with its punishing schedule of work and equally punishing night life.

The affair with Ava was conducted in the full glare of the media spotlight, and the resulting

adverse publicity destroyed what remained of Sinatra's career. While the public enjoyed the spectacle of two of their idols behaving in a way that probably most of them secretly envied, morality also dictated that they should pay – and be seen to pay – the price for their blatant transgression of the code of public conduct. Twenty years later, the Sinatra/Gardner courtship and marriage would probably have served to enhance both their images and careers, but in the atmosphere of the Fifties there could only be one outcome. Perhaps if George Evans, Sinatra's adroit and faithful press agent, had been alive, he might have been able to contain some of the more excessive activities of the couple and the ensuing publicity. But, in January 1950, Evans died of a heart attack.

The affair, begun in New York, ranged widely and with a total lack of reticence on the couple's part, as if they were quite deliberately courting the adverse publicity they inevitably received. When Sinatra went to sing at the Shamrock Hotel in Houston at the end of January 1950, Ava went too and they were seen dining together in a Houston restaurant with the mayor, although they refused to be photographed. Sinatra later admitted that the trip had been: 'A major mistake. But I was so in love I didn't care how it looked, having her there while I was still married.' Nancy, however, did care. In February, it was announced by columnist Hedda Hopper that Sinatra had moved out of their home on Valentine's Day.

For Sinatra, worried about his career, his appearance at the Copacabana in New York at the end of March was important – and it went sour. He and Ava had both taken suites at the Hampshire House in New York, only adding to the adverse press they were both receiving. He needed treatment for a throat condition before going on stage to find that the Sinatra magic had evaporated. Instead of having the audience

under his control, at one point he was forced to say to them, 'This is my opening night. Give me a chance.' And, when he sang 'Nancy With The Laughing Face' – a song written for his daughter, not his wife – audience reaction was too predictable. They laughed and turned to stare at Ava. Critical response to the engagement was equally unfavourable and it soon became clear during recording sessions held at the time that Sinatra's voice was under great strain.

'**H**e was so wild, so full of love and energy that he was like three men rolled into one. But behind the front of a big drinker and party-giver, he is highly sensitive and intelligent – and he has a heart of gold.'

AVA GARDNER

No more so than his stormy relationship with Ava. The Hampshire House became noted for their battles, as Ava was unable to give Sinatra the strength he needed to carry on at the Copacabana. She had her own career to think about and was preparing to fly to Spain to begin filming *Pandora and the Flying Dutchman* for MGM. Finally, she turned to her former husband Artie Shaw for help, triggering off one of the most bizzare events in the highly public courtship. When Sinatra found out whom she had gone to, he tried to locate the couple. When that failed, he threatened to kill himself, so it was reported, firing two shots from a pistol for which he had a permit into a hotel mattress. By the time the police arrived, there were no holes to be seen: the mattress had been exchanged. The incident did serve to underline Sinatra's seriousness about the affair however.

In April, Nancy Sinatra filed for separate maintenance: there was, the press was told, no

question of a divorce. The following day there *was* a divorce, however, as MGM and Sinatra parted company, ostensibly at Sinatra's request, although clearly the studio was far from happy about the adverse publicity surrounding two of its stars, to say nothing of Sinatra's battles for better roles. The only Sinatra movie left in the pipeline was a dire film he had made for Howard Hughes, co-starring him with Jane Russell and Groucho Marx. Filmed in 1948, it was so bad that it failed to get a release until 1951, under the title *Double Dynamite*–which had nothing to do with Sinatra and the plot, but everything to do with its leading lady.

Sinatra continued to woo Ava by telephone from New York when she finally went to Spain for *Pandora and the Flying Dutchman*. He came under increased strain when reports began to filter back of an alleged romance between Ava and bull-fighter Mario Cabre, who had a small role in the film–as Ava's lover. Strain probably caused him to lose his voice altogether when he suffered a sub-mucosal haemorrhage, and was replaced at the Copacabana by the man who had ousted him in the *Down Beat* poll–Billy Eckstine.

Ignoring his doctor's advice, Sinatra provided the media with yet another beanfeast by flying to Spain to be with Ava, taking with him the gift of an emerald and diamond necklace. Reporters laid siege to Ava's rented villa and hounded him for a statement–any statement. They followed the couple around when they went shopping. The immense and hostile publicity only served further to erode what was left of Sinatra's popularity. He flew back to the United States and returned to the Holmby Hills house to talk with Nancy and to bring presents for the children.

His career received a minor fillip when Bob Hope gave him a spot on his television special and, in July 1950, when he made his debut at the London Palladium, his ego received yet another and badly needed boost. His throat had healed and his reception was ecstatic, including adulation from screaming teenage girls of the sort he had thought, from his recent American experiences, had long since vanished. Not only was the audience–which included Ava sitting in the centre of the front row on his opening night–all for him, but so were the press. Said *Musical Express*, 'I watched mass hysteria. Was it wonderful? Decidedly so, for this man Sinatra is a superb performer and a great artiste. He had his audience spellbound. . . .' And, even more satisfyingly, the press in Britain concentrated on Sinatra the performer. Although he was living in a rented apartment in Berkeley Square and Ava in a flat nearby while she finished studio interiors at MGM's Boreham Wood Studios for *Pandora and the Flying Dutchman*, the media, with true British reticence, left them alone.

On his return to America, Sinatra was soon conscious that the Palladium date had been merely a temporary respite. His record sales continued to fall and Mannie Sachs, his friend and some-time mentor, had been replaced at Columbia Records by Mitch Miller. There was no empathy between the two men, particularly as Miller ruled his artists with a rod of iron and forced Sinatra to sing songs totally unsuited to his style. He was still unable to adapt to the new hard-hitting delivery and style of the 'beat' singers who had usurped his position in the public favour.

In September 1950, Nancy won her suit for separate maintenance, receiving, among other items, the Holmby Hills house in which she still lives. The way seemed clearer for Sinatra and Ava finally to be married, although it would be another year before they could actually do so.

♪IT'S OVER, IT'S OVER, IT'S OVER♫

Meanwhile, Sinatra's downward slide continued without check. His television debut on CBS failed to win ratings or please the critics. Said *The New York Times*, 'Sinatra walked off the TV high dive but unfortunately fell into the shallow end of the pool.' Record sales went on dropping, a situation that was exacerbated by two factors. The first was that in 1951 Sinatra only attended six recording sessions, being more preoccupied with his pursuit of Ava. The second was more serious still: the mutual and violent antipathy which had developed between Mitch Miller, Columbia's new Artists and Repertoire manager, and Sinatra.

In a year when Johnny Ray, Rosemary Clooney, Guy Mitchell, and Tony Bennett all produced hit songs for Miller, Sinatra made the worst record of his career: a duet with blonde 'singer' Dagmar and some singing dogs, a novelty number called 'Mama Will Bark'. Miller had claimed that the session with Dagmar would boost Sinatra's record sales. It did not. Later, when Miller offered Sinatra the songs 'My Heart Cried For You' and 'The Roving Kind', Sinatra refused to record them and left the session. Guy Mitchell made them both into major hits.

With the loss of sponsors on both radio and television, Sinatra accepted a three-year non-exclusive contract with Universal and made his first (and only) film for them in 1951, *Meet Danny Wilson*. Its plot owed more to Sinatra's public image than to Don McGuire's screenplay as it depicted the rise of a big-headed crooner, with the help of gangsters. Despite nine songs from Sinatra, the box-office response was indifferent. *Time* drew the inevitable parallel: '*Meet Danny Wilson* pictures the rise of a brash but likeable crooner to the special fame that only bobby-soxers can bestow. Apart from romantic and melodramatic trimmings that it borrows elsewhere, the story cribs so freely from the career and personality of Frank Sinatra that fans may expect Ava Gardner to pop up in the last reel.'

In fact, by the time the review appeared in 1952 Ava Gardner had become Mrs Frank Sinatra in real life. Throughout 1951, Sinatra had been under constant pressure from Ava to obtain a divorce. Finally Nancy, realising that the marriage was completely beyond repair, decided, Catholic or not, to apply for a divorce. She obtained her decree in California at the end of October 1951. Meanwhile, Sinatra had used singing engagements in Nevada to establish residence in the state and he received his divorce from Nancy on 1 November. The financial wranglings that had accompanied the divorce settlement left him almost broke, and emotionally the toll had been tremendous, affecting both him and Ava.

The couple were married in Philadelphia on 7 November. Ava was given away by Mannie Sachs and the wedding took place at the home of his cousin, with Axel Stordahl, Sinatra's arranger-conductor, as best man. Despite their attempts to keep the wedding ceremony private, the proceedings were marred by the almost ritual encounter with the press. Sinatra was reported as shouting at the assembled pressmen, 'How did those creeps know where we were? I don't want no circus here. I'll knock the first guy who tries to get inside on his ass — and I mean it!' It was an inauspicious start to the marriage and things did not fare much better on the three-day honeymoon the couple took before Sinatra had to return to New York for his television show. The projected three days in Havana turned into two when the couple had to wait in Miama overnight in order for their luggage to catch up with them. It was only after the marriage had broken up that it was made public that Ava had to pay for the honeymoon, because of Sinatra's desperate financial straits.

The marriage developed into a continuation of the rows and heated arguments that had marked their courtship. Only four months after the wedding, a film-fan magazine was headlining an article: 'THE BATTLING SINATRAS'. The fact was that Sinatra was finding it extremely difficult not only to adjust to his disintegrating career but also to accept that he was now married to a woman who was eminently successful in her own right. In December 1951, Sinatra and Ava flew to London for a charity concert at the Palladium, sponsored by the Duke of Edinburgh. Sinatra appeared with over one hundred American and British stars and, in stark contrast to his previous Palladium appearance, this time the response was only mild. It was a chilling omen for 1952, the year in which he would touch rock bottom. To add to his miseries, their hotel room was burgled:

among the items stolen was a gift of jewelry he had given Ava during the filming of *Pandora and the Flying Dutchman*.

By 1952, Sinatra was willing to do almost anything to revive his career, even to appearing in a totally unconvincing role, that of a humble and truly penitent man concerned only with the healing of old wounds and establishing a new rapport with the press. He was quoted as saying, 'I lost control of my temper and said things. They were said under great stress and pressure. I'm honestly sorry', and 'I'm a highly emotional person. I do things on the spur of the moment.' But the Sinatra who offered these and other similar placebos was neither credible nor newsworthy and the campaign failed.

Although *Meet Danny Wilson* was not a Paramount film, Sinatra and his advisers succeeded in persuading the management of the theatre to play the movie while Sinatra appeared live on stage, at the scene of his previous triumphs. This time was to be strikingly different. Not only were there no scenes of crowd hysteria, the engagement itself was a failure,

with empty seats and tepid press reaction. Ava, held up on the shooting of the film *The Snows of Kilimanjaro*, despite assurances that work would be completed in time for her to fly to New York, missed Sinatra's Paramount opening. It was another major jolt to an already shaky marriage. And, when she accompanied Sinatra to his next engagement, at the Chez Paree nightclub in Chicago, she was witness to yet another low, as Sinatra failed to draw audiences.

Professionally, Ava was going from strength to strength, with her performance in *The Snows of Kilimanjaro* making her into a top international star. It was ironic and not a little galling for Sinatra, who found his own career falling to pieces around him. By the end of the year he would have nothing to prevent him from accompanying Ava to Africa for location work on the film *Mogambo*. Nothing, that is, except for a particular part in a particular film.

♪WHEN NO ONE CARES♩

First to go was his television contract, cancelled by CBS when the shows failed to find either sponsors or audiences. Then Universal, seeing the tepid reception given to *Meet Danny Wilson*, announced that they did not intend to pick up Sinatra's option with the studio. Far more serious, however, in its implications and in its effect on Sinatra was the firing by his agency, MCA. They claimed that he owed them some $40,000 in back commissions, a figure disputed by Sinatra. But, whether or not that was the figure, the ugly truth was MCA no longer wanted to represent him. Said Sinatra, 'The hurt was deep and lasting. Can you imagine being fired by an agency that never had to sell you?' Then came the ultimate blow. 1952 marked the tenth and final year of his contract with Columbia. They did not wait until the end of the year or for Sinatra to fulfil his contractual obligations: the contract was not renewed and Sinatra cut his final disc for them on 17 September. Ironically, its title was 'Why Try To Change Me Now?' Sinatra left Columbia owing them some $100,000, which had been advanced to him against future royalties. As

things turned out, they were not going to have a long wait before recouping their money.

With all the pressures that were bearing down on Sinatra and Ava, it is hardly surprising that the year was marked by frequent and violent outbursts of marital discord. The most placid of marriages would have suffered badly under these sorts of stresses and theirs was anything but a placid relationship. Both possessed violent and volcanic tempers and both were extremely jealous people.

There was a series of well-publicised rows, estrangements, and equally public reconciliations, one at a campaign rally for Democratic presidential candidate Adlai Stevenson in Las Vegas. The crowd who turned out for the rally probably did so not because of Stevenson's presence, but rather to see whether Sinatra and

Ava would be there, and, if so, what would happen. The actuality was something of an anticlimax. Ava came up to the microphone and said, 'I can't do anything myself. But I can introduce a wonderful, wonderful man. I'm a great fan of his myself. Ladies and gentlemen, my husband, Frank Sinatra.' For the moment, all was well again with the Battling Sinatras. After the Stevenson rally, they took a trip to North Carolina to visit Ava's parents, and then flew together to East Africa, where Ava was due to start location filming on *Mogambo*.

Malindi is a small fishing village some eighty miles north of the port of Mombasa on Kenya's seaboard. In the Fifties, it was also a fairly inaccessible holiday resort, noted for its superb beach and excellent surfing. Most people who stayed there were local East Africans on holiday, living in wide verandahed holiday homes set back from the beach among groves of coconut palm and lush tropical vegetation. For the more wealthy and then infrequent tourists, Malindi also possessed one luxury hotel. This was the Eden Roc, which proclaimed its luxury status by having its own swimming pool, standing somewhat redundantly only a few yards away from the breakers coming into the beach.

I was spending part of my school holidays there, staying with friends. Early one morning I walked down from the house to find a powerfully built man sunning himself on the beach. Surprisingly, the man reminded me forcefully of someone I knew well, although I had never met him.

'You look just like Clark Gable,' I told him.

'I am,' came the quite astonishing reply.

In a country without television, the cinema was our most popular form of entertainment, providing images of near mythical quality. Overawed, I accompanied the friendly and entertaining Clark Gable along the beach to the Eden Roc. Getting a piece of paper and a ballpoint pen, he gave me his autograph. During the space of a heady and near-unbelievable hour, I met members of the cast and crew of *Mogambo*. I remember Ava Gardner

as a woman of such stunning beauty that she appeared even more unlikely in the flesh than she had done, giant sized, on the movie screen. I was no film buff then and so most of the people I met meant nothing to me, not even the somewhat remote and ladylike blonde who managed to look immaculate among the flies, mosquitos, and heat of the East African coast. In fact, I didn't even try to get Grace Kelly's autograph.

I did recognise, however, the figure at the upright piano that stood at the rear of the Eden Roc's spacious verandah lounge, although it took me a while. He sat loosely, picking out notes with a single finger, and smoking. He was unshaven, clearly far from happy, and he wore nothing except a pair of bathing trunks. I suggested to my host that I should ask him for his autograph. Clark Gable said that it would

be easier all round if he were to get it for me. I still have that autograph, a complicated and ornamental signature which reads 'Frank Sinatra'.

The next day, like something out of a movie, the guests had all departed, presumably to continue filming *Mogambo*. The Eden Roc returned to its former, unglamourous state, and I was left with a treasured sheet of paper and three autographs. It was many years later that I realised I had seen Frank Sinatra literally at the lowest point in his life. During the time he spent with Ava in East Africa, while she starred with Gable in *Mogambo*, his future literally hung on one single decision that would be made in Hollywood, by Harry Cohn, the head of Columbia Pictures. That day in Malindi, he was still waiting.

Eternity and After

If there is any single episode in Sinatra's life and career which has genuinely mythic stature, it is the fight for the role of Private Angelo Maggio in *From Here To Eternity* and the effect it was to have on his future. The event has become part of the lore of show business, surrounded by more legend and speculation than anything else.

'For the first time in my life I was reading something I really had to do. I just felt it, I knew I could do it, and I just couldn't get it out of my head.' This was Sinatra, referring to the character of Private Maggio, the doomed victim of the sadistic sergeant in James Jones's best-selling novel about army life just before the Japanese attack on Pearl Harbor.

♪WRAP YOUR TROUBLES IN DREAMS♪

Sinatra desperately wanted the part of Maggio and was willing to do anything in order to get it. He knew that it could establish him as a serious actor, something his playing of the priest in *Miracle of the Bells* had failed to do. Unfortunately, Columbia Pictures, who had purchased the novel for filming, did not share Sinatra's belief, despite his intense lobbying. It was hardly surprising since there was nothing in his previous screen career to indicate that he could handle a totally dramatic part. In any case, the tough Columbia studio head, Harry Cohn, had already announced that he wanted Eli Wallach for Maggio.

The announcement about Wallach failed to deter Sinatra from mounting an all-out attack on Columbia to get the part he so desperately needed. He got Ava to see the notoriously unsympathetic Cohn and, when that ploy had no apparent effect, Ava approached Cohn's wife Joan to see if she could intercede with her husband on Sinatra's behalf. That, too, failed.

Meanwhile, the original producer, Sylvan Simon, died and Buddy Adler was assigned to the film. Sinatra knew him and went to him to plead for the part. Adler, seeing Sinatra only in the role of a singer, told him that it was an acting part and remained unmoved by his pleadings.

Finally, in one last desperate attempt, Sinatra engineered a meeting with Cohn himself. He was not unknown to the man who prided himself on being one of the biggest bastards in Hollywood. Some years previously Sinatra had done Cohn a favour by asking for a dire Columbia movie, *Miss Grant Takes Richmond*, to be featured during one of his theatre appearances, something that had undoubtedly helped both the movie and Columbia. Characteristically, however, Sinatra did not remind Cohn of this fact when they finally met at lunch.

Reportedly, when Sinatra begged for the role, Cohn told him, like Adler before him, that Maggio was an actor's part. 'You're a singer,' he continued, 'Not an actor. We want an actor.' Even though it became clear that Cohn was not listening to his arguments, Sinatra continued to plead with him, telling Cohn that the role of Maggio might have been written for him, that he *knew* Maggio from his own experiences growing up in Hoboken and his Italian-American background, and throwing in just about every other argument he could think of. Cohn remained unmoved.

A Star is Born–*again*! Sinatra's 'comeback' performance in *From Here To Eternity* wins him the Oscar for Best Supporting Actor. Two scenes from the movie, with Montgomery Clift as Robert E. Lee Prewitt, and an off-set shot (*bottom right*) as co-stars Clift, Burt Lancaster, and Sinatra take a break

home affairs. As his career picks up, Sinatra's
marriage to Ava begins to break down, accompanied
by the sort of media publicity that had characterised
their stormy courtship. (The *Daily Mail* report
appeared on 9 September, 1953.) The progressive
strains of their deteriorating relationship show up
only too clearly on their faces

MISS AVA GARDNER, the film actress, and her crooner husband Frank Sinatra are living in separate New York hotels. They have not spoken to each other since Miss Gardner arrived back from Europe yesterday.

Miss Gardner said she would not attend her husband's opening at the night club Riviera in New Jersey tonight. She said: "I'd be most happy to see Frank, but he's got to make the first move."

Finally, Sinatra took a gamble. He broached the subject of money, banking on Cohn's well-known miserliness when it came to paying actors. If even half the legends about this particular confrontation are true, next to Maggio, Sinatra's best performance was the one he put on for Harry Cohn. Cohn rose to the bait, particularly after Sinatra informed him that he had been receiving $150,000 a film, only, as expected, to be told that that had been in the past. What sort of money was Sinatra expecting to be paid for playing Maggio, assuming quite hypothetically that he would be given the role? Sinatra swallowed pride and precedent. He told Cohn that he was willing to play the role for what amounted to his expenses–the ludicrous sum of $1,000 a week.

Cohn made no promises. He told Sinatra that,

apart from Wallach, there were other actors– *real* actors, he stressed characteristically–who were still to be tested, though of course the part was Wallach's, regardless of the outcome of any screen tests. Clearly, however, the chance to budget the role at a mere $1,000 a week for eight weeks must have been a totally irresistible proposition to Cohn. Still he let Sinatra go off with Ava to Africa.

Once there, Sinatra not only failed to hear anything from Columbia, but also found himself involved with a major MGM movie in which his role was simply that of spectator and husband of the star. Inevitably, the rows between him and Ava became more frequent and more bitter. Although they would not separate for another ten months or so and would not divorce until 1957, their marriage was by now almost over

The Capitol Years–from 1953 to 1960–marked the emergence of Sinatra as the romantic singer *par excellence* and master of the long-playing record. With Capitol chief Glen Wallichs (*right*); with Nelson Riddle (*below right*), his greatest arranger, alongside whom Sinatra cut over two hundred Capitol titles; and the studio Sinatra, relaxed, controlled, and happy (*opposite*)

as two extremely passionate and temperamental people rubbed each other's nerves raw.

Then, just before Christmas 1952, Sinatra received a cable telling him to report to Columbia to screen test for Maggio. Cohn's miserly instincts had triumphed, to the extent that Sinatra himself had to pay for the flight to Hollywood, reaching the studios thirty-six hours after getting Adler's cable. His was the last test of the day. Adler was summoned down to the sound stage by director Fred Zinnemann who told him, 'You'd better come down here. You'll see something really unbelievable. I already have it in the camera. I'm not using film this time, but I want you to see it.' What Adler and Zinnemann saw convinced them that Sinatra had been right: Maggio *was* Sinatra. But Cohn's final approval was still needed, despite the fact that, unknown to Sinatra, Wallach had had to turn down the part because of a previous stage commitment. Neither producer nor director told him just how good he had been. Not that that mattered to Sinatra: he *knew*.

Borrowing money from a friend for presents for Ava (whose birthday fell on Christmas Eve), Sinatra flew back to East Africa in a jubilant mood and for a while the Battling Sinatras ceased to battle. At first nothing, not even the news that Ava had had to fly to London where she had a miscarriage while he was in Hollywood, could affect Sinatra's euphoria. Then, as time passed with no news from Columbia, the quarrels and bitterness began again.

♪ POCKETFUL OF MIRACLES ♫

Finally the break came, the culmination of Sinatra's obsessive campaign. He was cabled and told that Maggio was his. He was poised to make the comeback that nobody–except Sinatra–could ever have expected. A week

When he's recording, the casual Sinatra with his 'one-take' attitude to movie-making vanishes to be replaced by the serious man of music, a total professional and complete perfectionist, willing to sing take after take until the sound is exactly what he wants. These recording sessions are by no means stuffy occasions, however—friends are welcome, as Lauren Bacall listens with him to playback (*below*)

after getting the cable, he returned to Hollywood not only to prepare for the filming of *From Here To Eternity* but also to rebuild the rest of his career. His first act was to sign with a new talent agency, the William Morris, and then he began looking for a new record company. Mannie Sachs had joined RCA Victor but was unable to persuade his colleagues to sign Sinatra. They were none too keen to take on an artist with so poor a recent track record, and,

moreover, one who owed $100,000 to his previous recording company and $109,996 in back taxes. And *From Here To Eternity* had still to be made. Finally, Sinatra was signed by Capitol records to a one-year contract after Dave Dexter, one-time editor of *Down Beat*, had persuaded his Capitol superior, Alan W. Livingstone. The contract was a tough one, with Sinatra receiving no advances and having to bear the recording costs himself. But even then,

his pride, the one quality which had never deserted him even when things were at their worst, made itself felt once more. He refused to accept Dexter as his producer. 'I won't work for him,' he said. 'He's the jerk who rapped my records in *Down Beat*. Who needs him?' And so a more placid producer, Voyle Gilmore, was found for him.

Before cutting his first side for Capitol, Sinatra flew to Hawaii for his eight-week stint

below The Man with the Golden Statuette. George Murphy looks on as Sinatra holds the Special Academy Award given in 1945 for *The House I Live In* (*top*), with Peggy Ann Garner and her Academy Award as Outstanding Child Actress. And The Big One (*bottom*): Sinatra and co-star and fellow Oscar winner Donna Reed with their awards for *From Here To Eternity*

opposite Happy Days Are Here Again!

on *From Here To Eternity*. Faced with competition from actors like Montgomery Clift and Burt Lancaster and a director who was a perfectionist, Sinatra surprised everybody involved in the making of the film with his dedication, his humility, and, above all, with his prowess as an actor. Said producer Buddy Adler, 'Frank dreamt, slept and ate his part. He has the most amazing sense of timing and occasionally he'll drop in a word or two that makes the line actually bounce. He never made a fluff, and this from a man who never really had any training.' So great was Sinatra's hold on the role that the crew began to call him Maggio. Sinatra had been right when he had said, 'I knew that if a picture ever was made, I was the only actor to play Private Maggio, the funny and sour Italo-American. I knew Maggio. I went to high school with him in Hoboken. I was beaten up with him. I might have been Maggio.' For director Fred Zinnemann, he was, and Zinnemann was quoted as saying: 'He played Maggio so spontaneously, we almost never had to re-shoot a scene.'

By the time he left Honolulu, Sinatra was his old cock-sure and confident self once more, convinced, rightly, that his career was on the rise. This upturn in his fortunes, however, was to mark a parallel and rapid deterioration in his marriage. The couple were together on his highly successful European tour in mid 1953, quarrelling constantly and so bitterly that on one occasion, in London, the tenants of their apartment block tried to have them evicted. Ava refused to accompany her husband back to America at the end of the tour, after completing studio interiors for her latest film, *Knights of the Round Table*, at MGM's British studios. Still deeply in love, Sinatra returned alone to New York.

This time his marriage was crumbling not because of his liaisons with other women but

because his wife was unable to compete with the one thing she had never had to face in their relationship previously – the fact that Sinatra's career was on the upturn and he no longer needed her emotional support to cushion him against a hostile world. 'When he was down and out,' she was quoted as saying, 'he was so sweet. But now that he's gotten successful again, he's become his old arrogant self. We were happy when he was on the skids.'

If her love for Sinatra had cooled, his for her had not and the year was marked by a series of reconciliations and estrangements. At the beginning of October, they went together to the New York premiere of *Mogambo*. Just over three weeks later, MGM announced their final separation, adding that Ava would be seeking a divorce. Sinatra's comment was: 'If it took seventy-five years to get a divorce, there wouldn't be any other woman' and certainly he appeared to carry a torch for Ava for a considerable time, even after the divorce which Ava obtained in Mexico on 5 July, 1957. But there never was the rumoured reconciliation and finally Sinatra assumed the role that was to be his until his next marriage – to Mia Farrow in 1966 – that of the world's most eligible bachelor, rich, successful, and happy with his reputation as one of Hollywood's great swingers.

Back in April 1953, Sinatra cut his first disc for Capitol with conductor-arranger Axel Stordahl, the rhythmic and gentle 'I'm Walking Behind You' and 'Lean Baby'. By the time the next session came around, Stordahl had accepted an offer to conduct and arrange for Eddie Fisher's television show. Gilmore, who was after a more swinging approach than the one achieved with Stordahl, suggested Billy May. When May was unable to make the session because of previous commitments, Gilmore suggested, and Sinatra accepted, Nelson Riddle. In his career as a singer it was as notable a milestone as Maggio was to prove in his movie work.

♪TOO MARVELLOUS FOR WORDS♫

The combination of Sinatra and Riddle was one of the finest in the history of popular music, producing records which today are still as vibrant, melodic, and deeply felt as when they were initially recorded. Between them, Sinatra and Riddle changed the crooner and one-time bobbysoxers' idol into a mature genius, the world's greatest singer of popular songs.

'**M**any credit me with being responsible for Frank's renaissance as a recording star. But – his great talent put him back on top. He gave me the incentive to write for him. Frank has great sensitivity to the contributions of the men behind the vocalist.'

NELSON RIDDLE

Between them too, with Sinatra's unique way with lyrics and Riddle's ability to create arrangements that were in themselves works of art, they effectively changed the nature of the popular song itself. Said Riddle, 'I look for the peak of a song and build to it. We're telling a story. It has to have a beginning, a middle, a *climax* and an ending.' In place of the soft lushness of the earlier Sinatra arrangements, Riddle substituted the driving and swinging rhythm that marks the finest Sinatra recordings. Theirs was a symbiosis of talents that was to create for Sinatra a new and even greater success as a singer. Even though Sinatra has worked with many other arrangers and conductors – among them Billy May, Gordon Jenkins, Neal Hefti, Don Costa, Count Basie, Robert Farnon, and Quincy Jones – his work with Riddle still remains the quintessential Sinatra

A Man Alone Time for meditation for Sinatra as spy and marksman in 1967's *The Naked Runner* (Sinatra Enterprises)

and marks in many ways the true apogee of his career as a singer.

There was an immense difference between Sinatra's approach to filming and recording. When he was filming, particularly when his power and influence were re-established, his work was even more notable for his short span of attention and his dislike of doing re-takes. He always claimed that the first take, which was the spontaneous one, was the best, and his directors found it difficult and often impossible to persuade him to return in front of the cameras for another. When he was cutting a disc, however, the reverse was always the case, with Sinatra willing to record take after take until he was satisfied with the final result.

'Working with him was always a challenge,' Riddle has said. 'And there were times when the going got rough. Never a relaxed man, as Nat Cole was, for example, he was a perfectionist who drove himself and everybody around him relentlessly. You always approached him with a feeling of uneasiness, not only because he was so demanding and unpredictable, but because all his reactions were so violent . . . this man is a giant. Not that there aren't other good singers around. But he has imagination and scope of the rarest. After all these years, there is no one who can approach him.'

Out of their first session came the superb 'My One and Only Love'. By the end of 1953, Sinatra was to have recorded 'Young at Heart' (on 9 December) and the classic album *Songs For Young Lovers*. In 1954 'Young at Heart' was picked by *Billboard* in their annual poll as the year's Number One record – it had sold a million. *Songs For Young Lovers* too had become a best-seller and Sinatra found his album *Swing Easy* starring as the top LP in the *Billboard* chart. *Metronome* named Sinatra Singer of the Year at the end of 1954 and he was also *Down Beat*'s Most Popular Male Vocalist.

Sinatra had risen again as singer and recording star: to mark the event, he took out an advertisement in *Billboard* to detail all his awards and all his current work in films. It was signed: 'Busy, busy, busy – Frank'.

♪LOOKING AT THE WORLD THRU' ROSE COLOURED GLASSES♪

But the final seal on Sinatra's return to the top had come on 25 March, 1954. Although he was nominally one of the movie's stars, Sinatra was more than happy to receive the nomination for the Academy Award for the Best Supporting Performance (Male) for 1953. The other nominees were Eddie Albert for *Roman Holiday*, Brandon de Wilde and Jack Palance for *Shane*, and Robert Strauss for *Stalag 17*. Sinatra, accompanied by Frank Sinatra Jr and by his daughter Nancy, sat at the back of Hollywood's Pantages Theater. When actress Mercedes McCambridge announced that Sinatra had won the Oscar, the theatre was rocked by one of its most thunderous ovations ever. He had proved that there was life after (apparent) professional death.

Only the absence of Ava in Spain marred the triumph. Sinatra was living a lonely bachelor existence, sharing an apartment with songwriter Jule Styne. Still, there was his ex-wife Nancy, with whom he had spent the previous evening, there were his children, and there was his mother, whom Sinatra telephoned in New Jersey after the ceremony.

Sinatra himself was under no illusions as to what he had achieved and what the golden statuette meant to him and his future. Later he was quoted as saying, 'The greatest change in my life came the night they gave me the Oscar. It's funny about that statue. You walk up on that stage as if you are in a dream and they hand you that little man before twenty or thirty

right Film Fun. Sinatra, David Wayne, and Skye Terrier Butch–who plays canine pal Joe–have fun between takes in *The Tender Trap*

opposite, below The bait to catch swinging bachelor Sinatra in *The Tender Trap* is Debbie Reynolds–no contest!

opposite, above Sinatra as Nathan Detroit in *Guys and Dolls*; Brando alias Sky Masterson rolls the dice

million people and you have to fight to keep the tears back. It's a moment. Like your first girl or your first kiss. Like the first time you hit a guy and he went down. I've heard actors kid about the Academy Awards. Don't believe them. It was the biggest moment in their lives.'

From Here To Eternity marked Sinatra's second encounter with the Oscar. The first time had been nearly a decade previously when his short film *The House I Live In* had received a special Academy Award in 1945. In the future, his association with the Oscar would be in his capacity as an entertainer: in 1963, Sinatra was the host for the 35th Annual Awards; in 1969, at the 42nd Annual Awards he sang 'Star'; and in 1970 and 1973, he presented special awards to Cary Grant and Rosalind Russell. When he finally received another award himself, at the 43rd Annual Awards Ceremony in 1971, it was in recognition of his many and notable acts of charity: Sinatra was given the coveted Jean Hersholt Humanitarian Award.

(Ironically, however, coming during a period when his films were distinguished only by their general mediocrity, with such offerings as *Marriage on the Rocks*, *Assault on a Queen* and *Cast a Giant Shadow*, Sinatra did 'receive' another Oscar. But the award was given to him in a totally fictional context when he appeared briefly as himself in the dismal and inept 1966 movie, *The Oscar*.)

Nearly a quarter of a century later, Sinatra is still involved in a career that, after a false 'retirement', seems to be as busy as ever. But it was his achievement in 1954 that consolidated once and for all his claim to be considered a legend in his own lifetime. Not only did he confound his critics by revitalising a career which had seemed totally and irrevocably moribund but, perhaps even more incredibly, he achieved this resurrection in a field in which, at best, he had had only brief and peripheral

experience. Now he was a star *and* actor.

Sinatra had given a compelling and deeply felt performance in *From Here To Eternity*, and the reviews reflected his sudden emergence as an actor. Said *Time*, 'Frank Sinatra does Private Maggio like nothing he has ever done before. His face wears the calm of a man who is completely sure of what he is doing as he plays it straight from Little Italy. . . .' *The New Yorker* referred to him as 'a first rate actor', as did *Newsweek*, who wrote, 'Sinatra can act when the mood is on him and when the writing is good', while the *Los Angeles Examiner*'s reviewer Ruth Waterbury said, '. . . he will be among the first next Academy time. He is simply superb, comical, pitiful, childishly brave, pathetically defiant. . . . Sinatra makes his death scene one of the best ever photographed.'

This sort of critical reaction, coupled with his Oscar, made Sinatra a hot movie property for the rest of the Fifties and he took full advantage of the situation, making some sixteen films between *From Here To Eternity* and the end of the decade. Clearly he was concerned to capitalise upon his newly-found eminence as an

Philanthropic Frank, the international communicator. In Israel (*opposite, above left*), Sinatra wears a 'Fool's Cap' for the dedication of an international student centre in his name at Jerusalem's Hebrew University in April 1978. In the Forties (*opposite, above right*) Sinatra 'sends' children in a Methodist orphanage in Virginia (photograph by Stanley Kubrick) and is equally at home in Paris with children during his 1962 world tour for charity (*opposite, below*) or talking with a blind girl the same year at Britain's Sunshine Home for the Blind in Northwood, Middlesex (*below*)

actor, and his popularity was additionally enhanced by his increasing success as a singer and recording artist with Nelson Riddle at Capitol. Success in one medium reinforced success in the other, although to begin with much of his new popularity came from records.

Sinatra basically is a mood singer, whose way with a lyric and whose elegant phrasing demands more than what he has called, probably based on the pressures of his days as a band singer and radio vocalist, 'three hard minutes of commercial music'. His re-entry into the field of recording fortunately coincided with the growth of long-playing records, which freed him from the demands of having to put songs over within tightly defined time limits. He and Riddle were able to experiment and to refine the Sinatra sound and to perfect the technique that was, in the Fifties, to give birth to such all-time classic albums as *Songs For Young Lovers*, *In The Wee Small Hours*, *Songs For Swinging Lovers*, *Only The Lonely* and the highly inaptly titled *No One Cares*.

The one thing that was absolutely certain about Sinatra between 1954 and the end of the decade was that people did care–a very large number of people, who bought his records, packed in to see him on personal appearances, and bought tickets for his films. By the end of 1955, he was making a clean sweep of all the magazine readers' polls as a vocalist. In the following year, he was voted the Musician's Musician in a poll carried out by *Metronome*, with the number of votes cast for him larger than the total of all the votes received by all the other poll nominees. 1957 saw him top the polls as the best male singer in *Down Beat* and *Metronome*, well ahead of every other contender. The Fifties were very good years for Sinatra the singer.

♪ALL THE WAY♪

He spent the rest of the decade working almost continually in every medium. This was not merely to consolidate his reborn career: it also appeared that hard and constant work might help him forget Ava. In any case, as Sinatra had found out during his lean years, public favour can be terrifyingly fickle. He was determined that he would never fall victim to a rapid change in public taste again. Constant and, in the movies, varied work, provided insurance against this eventuality.

His first role after Maggio was as Baron, would-be presidential assassin in the minor thriller *Suddenly* (1954). The film was not a box-office success but it did confirm Sinatra's stature and versatility as an actor, causing *Cue*

right Sinatra as *Pal Joey*, 'the heel trapped between two bosom pals', here with Kim Novak. (The other pal was Rita Hayworth.) For the record, the dog is called Snuffy

below For once, Sinatra isn't displaying his boredom with the longeurs of film-making but emulating director Otto Preminger for *The Man With The Golden Arm*

opposite With his idol at last: Well, Did You Evah? Sinatra and Crosby in *High Society*

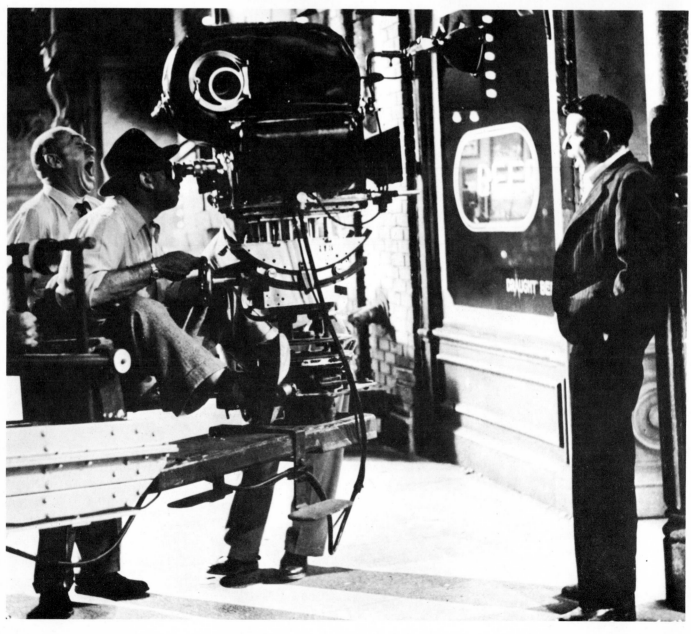

to remark, 'In *Suddenly*, Sinatra bears a full load as its star and dominating character. He holds the screen and commands it with ease, authority, and skill that is, obviously, the result of care, study, work and an intelligent mind.' Sinatra then joined the all-star cast—Robert Mitchum, Olivia de Havilland, Gloria Grahame, and Broderick Crawford—in Stanley Kramer's film version of Morton Thompson's best-selling novel about medical life, *Not As a Stranger* (1955). Again, as Mitchum's buddy, Sinatra, in a light but impressive performance,

received good reviews, among them *The Holly-wood Reporter*'s comment, 'Sinatra, who seems to become a better actor with each successive part, is simply terrific.' He was teamed with his one-time co-star from radio's 'Your Hit Parade', Doris Day, in *Young at Heart* in 1955, in which he sang the hit title-song, along with 'Someone to Watch Over Me', 'Just One of Those Things' and 'One for My Baby'.

His big move towards major screen stardom came when he returned to MGM, the studio which had once let him go, to make *The Tender*

Clan gatherings. Hank Henry, Dean Martin, Sammy Davis Jr, Sinatra, Richard Bakalayan, and two generations of Crosbys, Bing and son Phil, in Sixties Clan movie *Robin and The Seven Hoods* (*below*). Anything for a pal: Sinatra and Martin together on television (*opposite, left*). Anything you can do . . . I can do better: the line-up–Martin, Sinatra, Peter Lawford, Davis, and Joey Bishop (*opposite, above right*), and the combined Sinatra and Martin families together on Martin's television Christmas show (*opposite, below right*). Left to right: Deana, Nancy, Tina, Dino, Gail. Frank, Claudia, Jeanne, Craig, Gina, and Ricci

Trap later in 1955. It was one of the easy bachelor roles with which he was to become associated in his lesser Sixties movies. The film, which had Sinatra slipping comfortably into the part of a New York Casanova finally brought to heel by an apparently naive young actress, was a box-office success, giving him another hit song '(Love Is) The Tender Trap' and a complimentary review from *The New York Times*'s Bosley Crowther: '. . . It catches the nervous, restless Frankie at the top of his comedy form. Indeed, it is probably in his timing that his excellence with the quip is achieved, and this leads one to wonder how much his training as a singer contributed to what he is.'

The Tender Trap was followed by the part of Nathan Detroit in the film version of *Guys and Dolls* (1956) and, without doubt, Sinatra was

'**W**hen Sinatra dies and goes to Heaven, the first thing he'll do will be to find God and yell at him for making him bald.'

MARLON BRANDO

the best thing in the movie. The worst, easily, was Marlon Brando in the role of Sky Masterson, would-be-seducer of Jean Simmons's Sergeant Sarah Brown of the 'Save a Soul' Mission. Sinatra had wanted the Sky Masterson part himself, and he and Brando had little love for each other. In particular, Sinatra had no patience with Brando's method of acting with its soul-searching and constant re-takes. He dubbed Brando 'Mumbles' and was heard to say, 'I don't buy this take and re-take jazz. The

key to good acting on the screen is spontaneity—and that's something you lose a little with each take.'

♪I HAVEN'T TIME TO BE A MILLIONAIRE♪

Within two years of *From Here To Eternity*, Sinatra was back on top, earning in excess of one million dollars annually, which, with his shrewd business investments, was eventually to make him into one of the wealthiest men in show business. He also became one of the most generous, as evidenced by his treatment of actor Lee J. Cobb, who suffered a heart attack at the time Sinatra was making *The Tender Trap*. Although they had met only briefly, when they worked together on *Miracle of the Bells*, Cobb found Sinatra a constant, and concerned,

hospital visitor, whose concern manifested itself when Sinatra paid Cobb's hospital bills and let the actor recover at his Palm Springs and Hollywood homes. This is a side of Sinatra's character that has been less publicised, perhaps because positive news is never as fascinating as negative, headline-hitting material, and also because Sinatra himself has not seen fit always to disclose his charitable acts. Nonetheless, they are legion and Sinatra eminently deserved the Jean Hersholt Humanitarian Award given him in 1971.

When Bela Lugosi committed himself for treatment for his drug addiction, it was Sinatra alone out of the Hollywood colony who befriended him and offered him support. When, some years later, George Raft found himself broke and facing massive demands for back taxes, Sinatra gave him a (literally) blank

cheque. In 1962, he undertook a gruelling three-month world tour to raise money for children's charities, a tour that cost almost one million pounds, every penny of which Sinatra himself paid. During 1970, in May and in November, he gave two charity concerts at London's Royal Festival Hall, which raised over £120,000 for children's charities. Nor was his charity confined to such large-scale activities. Learning in 1970 that Dan Mitrione, an American kidnapped and killed in South America, had left a widow and nine children, Sinatra set up a benefit show in the gymnasium of Mitrione's home town in Indiana, with himself, Jerry Lewis, and a rock group: the show raised over $100,000 for Mitrione's widow and family. And, when a 71-year-old English woman found herself stranded in the States in 1972 without funds, Sinatra sent her the money for her air ticket back to Britain. Her comment: 'I have always been one of Mr Sinatra's greatest fans, but I never imagined he would be so thoughtful towards a little old lady in trouble.' And, in 1978, when ex-world heavyweight boxing champion Joe Louis had to undergo expensive open-heart surgery, it was Sinatra again who stepped in and paid the medical bills.

'He has the biggest heart in all the world. He's just the greatest person I've known.'

DORIS DAY

Returning to the mid Fifties and his busy film career, this period also saw Sinatra sue producer Sam Spiegel for allegedly breaking an oral agreement to give him the lead in *On The Waterfront*, the role that had gone to Marlon Brando, a fact which had no doubt only served to exacerbate the friction between the two men on the set of *Guys and Dolls*. But *Guys and Dolls* was followed by *The Man with the Golden Arm* (1956), probably the best and most challenging assignment of his whole film career, except for Maggio. His performance as Frankie Machine,

the poker dealer with the 'golden arm' struggling to cure himself of drug addiction, was powerful and convincing, and earned Sinatra a nomination for Best Actor, the Academy Award going in the end to Ernest Borgnine for *Marty*. And the reviews were good, with Sinatra being totally accepted as an actor–not as an ex-crooner, or as a singer turned screen performer. Said Arthur Knight in *The Saturday Review*, 'No small part of the complex emotional colouration we feel towards Frankie Machine comes from a truly virtuoso performance by Frank Sinatra. ... Indeed he brings to the character much that has not been written into the script, a shade of sweetness, a sense of edgy indestructibility that actually creates the appeal and intrinsic interest of the role. But he is also an actor of rare ability. ...' *Cue* agreed: 'It's quite a performance Frankie gives–and something of a revelation too.'

In dramatic terms, the rest of the decade's films were something of an anticlimax. In August 1955, Sinatra went to Maine to begin shooting *Carousel* for Twentieth Century-Fox. His stint on the film lasted only a few days

left It's So Nice To Go Trav'lin. Sinatra and his mobile status symbol, his Dual-Ghia

below More High Society: Sinatra and one-time co-star Grace Kelly, now Princess Grace of Monaco, hold hands at a party in Monte Carlo in 1958

because he refused point blank to make two films for the price of one, his way of explaining what Twentieth Century-Fox had in mind. They had intended that the film should be shot both in CinemaScope and Todd A-O, with the actors performing each scene twice, once for each camera system. Sinatra left the picture to be replaced by Gordon MacRae as the leading man, but the point had been made and taken and the film was finally shot in one process only. While he was embroiled with *Carousel*, Sinatra made the cover of *Time* magazine for the first time, as well as *Look*.

Sinatra's first movie as an independent producer was the rather silly Western, *Johnny Concho* (1956), which he filmed around his fortieth birthday. It was a flop. His next film, however, united him with his great idol, Bing Crosby, in the musical comedy *High Society*.

THE VOICE

by THE L

Lauren Bacall, who recently has been dating Frank Sinatra, tells FRANK COLLINS how she feels about the new man in her life

IT'S Hollywood's most talked-about romance. But, until now, it's been other people who have done the talking. For Frank Sinatra. The Voice, and Lauren Bacall, who once was dubbed The Look, have been silent. Now? Miss Bacall, widow of Humphrey Bogart, is at last talking about the new man in her life. .

"Everybody wants to know if I am going to marry again—and, mainly, whether I'm going to marry Frank. They should know right now that I am not the announcing type.

"I admit I date Frank more often than any other man, but I have dated others. They just don't get as much publicity. And I think I date Frank more often than other men because I am happy with him. I enjoy myself.

"We laugh and bubble a little at what we see and hear. And he is so full of surprises. Nothing pleases him more than to see a look of consternation on my face.

"For example, quite often we'll go out on a date and I'll ask Frank where we're going. With an absolutely poker face he'll answer: 'Oh, why don't we just have dinner over at the Capri and see a play?' I'll agree.

"Twenty minutes later, we walk into the Villa Capri and he steers me straight into the private dining-room. He opens the door, I walk in and twenty people whom I haven't seen in ages look up and say: 'Hi Betty! Long time no see!' You couldn't possibly know what that means to me."

About Sinatra's attraction to a woman, Miss Bacall says: "When he's with you, it seems as though there's no one else in the world but you. He adores you. As a man, he is just about the most charming, compassionate male a woman would want. He's witty and he's fun.

"Most people, however, get the mistaken idea that Frank wants the companionship of a woman to satisfy a need in his own character. That isn't true. Frank possesses a forceful personality. He

does want to be boss, but he doesn't regard it as a right—more as a privilege. And he is willing to earn it."

In the early stages, Sinatra dated Miss Bacall only with other couples—once with Mr. and Mrs. Sam Goldwyn, once with Lucille Ball and Desi Arnaz and other notable Hollywood couples. Then they started going around alone.

Sinatra's comments on the romance are in general terms non-committal. Says he: "I believe in giving a woman a lot of time to make up her mind about the guy she wants to spend the rest of her life with." And he doesn't like "hunters." "The male just doesn't like being crowded with female claustrophobia," he says.

Some American reports have said that Miss Bacall and Sinatra have now split up. But whether or not this is true, Miss Bacall has proved just how realistic is her summing up of the Sinatra character—and his widely reported reputation.

For, asked if she was dating Sinatra so much in an effort to change him before they married, she said: "Any woman who tries to change a man, particularly after he's reached his thirties, is a fool. She can only make him worse.

"I was married eleven years to a guy I still think is the finest man I have ever known. But you may be surprised to learn that I was tougher to live with than he was."

A few months ago, "because it held too many memories," she left the 300,000-dollar home she and Bogart had built.

And, now talking about herself as well as Sinatra, Lauren Bacall says: "I am not over sophisticated and I would feel very uncomfortable being regarded as one of those women who wants to go it alone."

She adds: "I hate loneliness."

Despite its vulgarisation of the play and film *The Philadelphia Story*, from which it derived, the movie was an immense popular success. He and Crosby were both first rate in their duet 'Well, Did You Evah?', and Sinatra's serenading of Grace Kelly showed him at his relaxed and melodic best. The film put Sinatra into the list of the Top Ten Money-Making Stars of 1956, at Number Nine, and he was to remain in the list until 1960.

The Pride and The Passion (1956) was made in Spain for Stanley Kramer, and Kramer soon fell foul of Sinatra's growing dislike of long-

shooting schedules or the need to be in one place for any length of time. In the end, it was Sinatra who won. Said Kramer, 'When Sinatra walks in a room, tension walks in beside him. You don't know why, but if he's tense, he spreads it.' He also said, 'Frank is a tremendously talented man, intuitive and fast, which is good for him but not always good for the other actors. During the filming of *The Pride and The Passion*, he didn't want to rehearse. He didn't want to wait around while crowd scenes were being set up. Eventually, for the sake of harmony, we shot all his scenes together and he

"Picturegoer" photograph of Frank Sinatra, Lauren Bacall by Hollywood cameraman Jay Scott

Between marriages, swinging Sinatra has been linked with just about every name in the Hollywood and jet-set book. Here's how the British movie magazine *Picturegoer* treated his romance with the widow of Rat Pack founder Humphrey Bogart

best as comedian Joe E. Lewis in *The Joker is Wild* (1957), but the film itself was a very ordinary biopic. Yet out of it came another hit for Sinatra in its Academy Award winning song, 'All The Way'. Sinatra had twenty-five per cent of *The Joker is Wild* and he also owned a percentage of his next film, Columbia's *Pal Joey* (1957). It was, to quote Sinatra, '. . . the only role I've dreamed of doing for many years outside of Private Maggio'. By the time the film emerged, John O'Hara's story of the nightclub singer who succeeds despite being an all-round heel had been suitably sanitised for movie audiences and Sinatra gave a performance that in no way showed Joey to be the second rater he was supposed to be. What made the film a particular treat for Sinatra fans was its score, which included such Rodgers and Hart classics as 'I Didn't Know What Time It Was', 'There's a Small Hotel', 'The Lady Is a Tramp', 'I Could Write a Book', and 'Bewitched, Bothered and Bewildered', and a swinging performance by one-time Columbia sex-goddess Rita Hayworth, here against Columbia's latest sex symbol, the wooden and untalented Kim Novak. *Look*, like the audiences, enjoyed the movie: 'Heading up an impressive cast,' it said, 'Frank Sinatra plays Joey with all the brass the role demands. He has a gleam in his eye and a chip on his shoulder, as he portrays this unsavoury character who could be so charming – against everybody's better judgement. He tosses off dames and songs with equal artistry and almost single-handedly makes *Pal Joey* a wonderfully entertaining movie.'

His 1958 movies were also run of the mill and *Kings Go Forth*, a heavy and melodramatic wartime romance which had Sinatra and Tony Curtis both fighting for the love of Natalie Wood, failed to make money, despite some lush French Riviera locations. By the time he came to make *Some Came Running*, all his casual attitudes to the actual process of film-making were fully established. Shooting began in the small Indiana town of Madison, where the behaviour of the film unit and particularly that

left early. The rest of the cast acquiesced because of the tension.' In fact, the film was just a piece of historical hokum, high on spectacle and low on characterisation, and Sinatra, as a Spanish patriot, looked and sounded highly unconvincing. Nevertheless, he received $250,000 for his work and the film made money.

♪OH! LOOK AT ME NOW♫

The rest of the films of the Fifties were nothing special, although they all scored at the box-office. Sinatra was at his acerbic wisecracking

below In a pensive mood during a recording session, the man once described by George Burns as 'the only singer in the world who sings like Frank Sinatra'

opposite Always the perfectionist, Sinatra seeks the ideal sound during a recording session

of Sinatra and co-star (and Clan member) Dean Martin alienated and angered the town's inhabitants, and when the unit returned to Hollywood to film the interiors, Sinatra instituted a noon-till-eight shooting schedule in place of the normal nine-till-five pattern. He just happened to prefer to work that way and such was his power now that MGM acquiesced: 'I got the idea for these hours in Europe. Performers work better in the afternoon. The girls look better and they don't run out of gas by five.' Sinatra was merely explaining away the fact that by now he would only make pictures *his* way and that was to a schedule that suited his own particular biorhythms. Critical response to the film was lukewarm, except for Shirley MacLaine's performance as the tart with the heart of gold befriended by author Sinatra, and the movie showed only too well

the constant off-screen battles that had taken place between its star and director Vincente Minnelli, out of his depth with cast and subject.

A Hole in the Head (1959) portrayed Sinatra as a widower with business problems, and it was slackly acted by its star and poorly directed by Frank Capra. However, one of the songs, 'High Hopes', written by Jimmy Van Heusen and Sammy Cahn, was a catchy beat number which won the Oscar for the Best Song of 1959. Sinatra's final film of the decade had the kid who had been turned down for military service playing a hard-drinking, tough American captain leading a guerilla band in Burma in World War Two in *Never So Few* (1959). The old 'War is Hell' story was put over competently enough by Sinatra and his fellow cast members but, like most of Sinatra's subsequent movies, with the honourable exception of *The Manchurian Candidate*, it was almost instantly forgettable.

What the film does provide, however, is a poignant demonstration of Sinatra's absolute power over his friends, associates, and entourage, and the total loyalty he demands of them. Originally, Sammy Davis Jr had been cast to play a role specially written for him in *Never So Few*. Then Sinatra heard rumours that Davis had slated him on a Chicago radio show. He checked the tape of the broadcast and heard Davis ad lib, 'I love Frank but there are many things he does that there is no excuse for . . . I don't care if you are the most talented person in the world. It does not give you a right to step on people and treat them rotten.' Davis lost the part (it was rewritten and played by Steve McQueen), and it was several months before a penitent Davis was forgiven and allowed to enter the charmed circle once more.

♪ JUST FRIENDS ♫

Sinatra's need for a constant and absolutely loyal circle of friends, acquaintances, but (above all) regular cronies was always to be a feature of his life, dating back to the time he lived near Humphrey Bogart in Holmby Hills. He had idolised Bogart for a number of years, liking in particular the star's sardonic and

dismissive attitude towards Hollywood and its essential phoniness and hypocrisy. As a result of this friendship Sinatra had found himself a member of a group of like-minded Hollywood people who tended to assemble informally either at Bogart's home or at Mike Romanoff's restaurant. Originally known as the Free Loaders, the group soon became dubbed the Rat Pack. Among its semi-regular membership were Judy Garland and her current husband Sid Luft, John Huston, Mike Romanoff, Swifty Lazar, David Niven, Betty Comden and Adolph Green, Nunnally Johnson, and Nathaniel Benchley as well as Bogart, Lauren Bacall, and Sinatra. This was the group that, after Bogart's death on 14 January, 1957, was to metamorphose into the far less lovable–and less loved–Sinatra Clan.

'**If Frank's your friend, then he's your friend for life. He'll go to endless trouble to get you out of a scrape. But if you make him your enemy – then I feel sorry for you.**'

VIC DAMONE

The difference between the two groups was very obvious. The Rat Pack was composed of basically kindred spirits. Behind the Clan lay the implicit assumption that its whole *raison d'etre* somehow derived from Sinatra, who was known variously as The Pope, The Dago, and Chairman of the Board. Patronage, rather than democracy, was its keynote and among the sometime members of the Rat Pack who were conspicuous by their absence were Lauren

Stargazer Sinatra as Mark Brittain in *Assault On A Queen* (Sinatra Enterprises-Seven Arts 1966)

Bacall, Katharine Hepburn, and Spencer Tracy. Instead, the numbers were made up by Dean Martin, Sammy Davis Jr, Peter Lawford, Joey Bishop, Tony Curtis, Sinatra's song writers Jimmy Van Heusen and Sammy Cahn, and Harry Kurnitz, while Shirley MacLaine, not a member, was held to be the Clan's mascot.

The loyalty demanded of its members by their leader was a two-way affair, however, and four of Sinatra's least successful Sixties movies, *Ocean's Eleven* (1960), *Sergeants Three* (1962), and *Four for Texas* and *Robin and the Seven Hoods* (both 1964), appeared mainly as elaborate excuses for the Clan to gather in front of the cameras and do whatever it was they enjoyed, to their obvious entertainment. Audiences, faced with what were basically lavishly mounted home-movies, found the films considerably less entertaining.

Throughout the Fifties, Sinatra kept up a busy schedule of personal appearances and concerts in addition to his movie-making and recording activities, and his nightclub performances once more showed him to be at the top of his form. The pattern was being set for the life style and career of the Sixties and Seventies, except that in 1970 Sinatra would make his last feature film to date, the abominable and unfunny comedy Western, *Dirty Dingus Magee*; he was not to go before the cameras again for another seven years, until in 1977 he made the television movie *Contract on Cherry Street.*

Only in romance were the Fifties in any way atypical of the swinging Sinatra of the Sixties and Seventies. For much of the decade he was nursing his still-glowing love for Ava, although in 1958 there were rumours that he and Humphrey Bogart's widow, Lauren Bacall, would marry, a rumour sedulously propagated by the Hollywood gossip columnist Louella Parsons, who announced exclusively 'SINATRA AND BACALL TO MARRY'. If there had been any such intention on either part, Louella Parsons's intervention killed it.

Later that year, however, Sinatra flew to London to act as master of ceremonies at the British premiere of the Danny Kaye picture, *Me and the Colonel*, his appearance raising some $70,000 for the British Cancer Fund. Sinatra's reception was all that he could have hoped for as the traffic around Leicester Square was brought to a standstill by chanting crowds anxious to get a glimpse of their hero. In the ten days or so between his arrival in Britain and the premiere, Sinatra met American-born Lady Adelle Beatty. Their meeting and subsequent encounters did not go unnoticed by the British press, who were less reticent this time in their handling of Sinatra, and only two days after his arrival the *Daily Mail* was announcing that Sinatra and Lady Beatty would marry.

All this press attention may have been the cause of Sinatra's somewhat bizarre announcement from the stage of the Odeon Cinema, Leicester Square, when, before introducing Kaye and the rest of the cast of *Me and the Colonel*, he told the audience, which included the Queen, 'I'm here in London solely for this film, the charity of tonight's showing and to introduce the cast. I did not come here to get married.' In excruciatingly bad taste he continued, 'Some of your newspapers would have me marry as often as King Farouk, and I'm not even as fat as he is.'

As events turned out, for the two years following their meeting, and until just before she married American film director Stanley Donen (who had co-directed Sinatra in *On The Town*), the romance appeared to be on as, announcing that she was off to the Bahamas, Lady Beatty would end up in Las Vegas, or Hollywood, or New York, or Miami – anywhere, in fact, where Sinatra just 'happened' to have a nightclub engagement.

Who Wants To Be a Millionaire?

Frank Sinatra is a unique phenomenon in show-business terms. In over forty years as an entertainer he has carved out not one but *two* legendary careers. The second continues unabated. It has been, to say the least, a considerable entertainment achievement.

Sinatra fought his way back to the top through a combination of sheer guts, dogged perseverance, and, although he himself tended to play down this particular aspect, through a great deal of luck, even if it was only the sort of luck that ensured that he was in the right place at the right time. By the end of the Fifties, he had built for himself a new and even greater career, one that he had consolidated beyond erosion. The catalyst for this new lease on his professional life was Maggio, of course, and, to a lesser extent, the brilliance of his recordings with Nelson Riddle, but all the impetus had come from Sinatra himself.

He, however, did not view his newly-found popularity as a comeback and was quoted as saying, 'It would be more accurate to call what happened to my career "the rise and fall and rise again of Frank Sinatra".' But *Variety*, in the person of its editor, Abel Green, was in no doubt, writing, 'It's the greatest come-back in theatre history. One good picture is all it takes. Now it's coming down in showers for Sinatra and everybody in show business is rooting for him.'

It is highly tempting to write about Sinatra's life and career after the Fifties in as much detail as before, but in many ways it would be a redundant exercise. All the elements of character and career which make Sinatra the unique person he is today were already present by the end of the Fifties. True, in the Sixties and Seventies much would happen to Sinatra, but all of it has been merely an extension of the second career he created for himself with *From Here To Eternity* and his Capitol recordings. To cover all these events would merely be to list a continuing stream of successes, and, while it is undeniably true that success breeds success, a mere cataloguing of achievements–however, impressive–finally ends up as nothing more than a series of milestones and chapter headings. Such an approach tends to bring out little that is new. Nor does it offer further insights into Sinatra's complex character.

I hope that the reason I have chosen to concentrate upon those years in which Sinatra was battling for success is obvious. In the creation of his two careers, I found dramatic and fascinating themes: once a position of unassailable success had been attained, it was no longer possible to discern a genuinely valid theme. Perhaps something more than the cliché of continuing achievement and the underscoring of an already established legend may be revealed in years to come.

The Sixties and Seventies have served to accentuate traits that already existed in Sinatra, notably his determination to be his own master. By 1960, Sinatra had already made himself into an extremely wealthy man. His financial empire, controlled by Sinatra Enterprises, included his record, music-publishing and movie interests, a considerable investment in real estate, interests in radio stations shared

In company: fooling around with Bop Hope on a
television show (*left*), and with another of the world's
great singers–the one and only Ella Fitzgerald (*below
left*)

with Danny Kaye, plus a small air-charter
outfit. In late 1964, alone, his wealth was
estimated at some $20,000,000. No wonder he
had looked relaxed in 1956, singing Cole
Porter's 'Who Wants To Be a Millionaire' with
Celeste Holm in the movie *High Society*. He had
made that status quite a few times over and
lived accordingly, with private jets and houses
and apartments wherever he needed them.

His next concern was to get the same measure
of creative autonomy as he had achieved
financially. In films and in personal appearances, this presented no problem. What Sinatra
now required was total independence from his
recording company, Capitol. So, in 1960, he did
his first session for his own record company,
Reprise Records, although it was not until the
following year that Reprise finally became
established, after legal hassles with Capitol.
Sinatra had what he had always wanted–total
control over his material, plus, of course,
ultimately a far greater financial return on his
labours.

The financial as well as the artistic motive
behind Sinatra's decision was evidenced by the
remark he is supposed to have made to Morris
Ostin, whom Sinatra made his vice-president at
Reprise. As they walked past the Capitol Tower
in Hollywood, Sinatra said, 'I helped build that.
Now, let's build one of my own.' His first album
with his own company was *Ring-a-Ding Ding*,
conducted and arranged by Johnny Mandel
since Nelson Riddle was still under contract to
Capitol.

♪ THE GOOD LIFE ♫

Sinatra's success with Reprise was something
he wanted to share and, at its inception, he took
advertisements in *Billboard* and *Variety* which
claimed, 'Now a newer, happier, emancipated
Sinatra ... untrammelled, unfettered, uncon-
fined ... on Reprise'. The motto: 'Reprise, to
play and play again'. And sales proved the
motto. Then again, in 1963, Sinatra under-
lined the fact that, as well as being an enter-

tainer, he was also an extremely astute businessman, when he sold two-thirds of his stock in Reprise to Warner Brothers, in a deal that involved a series of films to be made for the studio, as well as several million dollars. It was even openly rumoured at the time that the boss of Warners, Jack L. Warner, saw Sinatra as a possible heir.

During the period between 1960 and 1970, the year he made *Dirty Dingus McGee*, his last feature film to date, Sinatra appeared in some twenty movies, although in some of them, such as the Hope and Crosby *Road to Hong Kong* (1962) and *Pepe* (1960), he was merely a guest. Most of these films were undistinguished, seeming to betray a lessening of Sinatra's interest in the medium beyond the casualness of his one-take method of movie-making. Certainly the best of them was the political thriller *The Manchurian Candidate* (1962), directed in bravura style by John Frankenheimer from Richard Condon's novel, with its uncanny parallels (before the event) with the assassination of John F. Kennedy. The film, however, proved a greater draw for the critics than for audiences.

In 1965, Sinatra produced, directed, and acted in *None But The Brave*, a war drama which also featured his (then) son-in-law Tommy Sands, who had married Nancy in 1960, divorcing her in 1965. Sinatra as director was competently anonymous and he seemed content to hand over the acting honours to Clint Walker. The most interesting events connected with the film took place off screen when, during location filming in Hawaii, actor Brad Dexter (the one no-one remembers on *The Magnificent Seven*) rescued Sinatra from drowning.

Dexter was rewarded by being made producer on the later Sinatra movie *The Naked Runner* (1967), made in Britain, although it was reported that he and the director, Sidney J. Furie, had to put it together with what material they had completed at the time Sinatra left the film. Certainly there was nothing about it to lure

people into the cinemas. Sinatra's casual approach was noticeable in most of these films, even in those which were not merely excuses for him and the Clan to work together, with *Von Ryan's Express* (1965), a prisoner-of-war escape movie in which Sinatra co-starred with a railway train, probably emerging as the most profitable.

The most interesting were the three detective movies, *Tony Rome* made in 1967, its 1968 sequel *Lady in Cement*, and the same year's *The Detective*. The first two featured him as a private eye operating out of Miami and his by now fairly battered features, world-weary appearance, and general air of cynicism gave the roles perhaps a greater depth than they actually contained. The style was there, a style based very much upon the Philip Marlowe and Sam Spade of Humphrey Bogart, although without the latter's existential charisma. Nevertheless, whatever their deficiencies, these movies were considerably better than some of the other films of the period such as *Robin and the Seven Hoods*, *Marriage on the Rocks* (1965), and *Assault on a Queen* (1966), films that looked as tired and listless as their star. *The Detective*, although setting Sinatra officially on the side of the law, still had him very much in the private-eye persona as he investigated a series of homosexual murders. The film did not possess much in the way of genuine style and it was hardly attractive to watch, but Sinatra's variation on the theme of the private eye was worth some attention. After the (deservedly) hostile press given to his 'comedy' Western *Dirty Dingus McGee*, Sinatra abandoned movies, although it was rumoured in 1974 that Paramount were trying to lure him back to the screen for *The Little Prince*. They failed.

It was in 1944, when he espoused the cause of the re-election of Franklin Roosevelt, that Sinatra received his first savaging at the hands of the press. Nevertheless, the political aspect of his character continued to be a powerful one. In 1960, he helped to campaign for the election of John F. Kennedy, giving the media plenty of

ammunition to use against him. They were not slow to do so, particularly now that Sinatra was eminently newsworthy and there was additional news value in the fact that the 'infamous' Clan was also heavily involved in the campaigning. This was hardly surprising since Clan member Peter Lawford was related by marriage to the President-to-be. The media kept up their attack on Sinatra right through the campaign and for a long time afterwards, inevitably contributing to the final break-up between Sinatra and the Democrats.

left Movie moment. Sinatra has a quiet off-set chat with associate producer Saul Chaplin during the filming of *Can-Can*

right, above Sinatra and Crosby enjoying themselves at a relaxed Reprise recording session

right, below Norman Lear directs Sinatra and Phyllis McGuire in a scene from the movie *Come Blow Your Horn*

Early in 1960, Sinatra offered them a perfect excuse for an onslaught: he announced that he had engaged Albert Maltz to write the screenplay of a projected movie, *The Execution of Private Slovik*. Maltz was one of the blacklisted 'Hollywood Ten' and had been jailed for refusing to testify about his Communist affiliations. The furore that broke about Sinatra's head came this time not only from the media but also from the Hollywood Establishment (notably John Wayne and publicist Russell Birdwell), veteran groups, Congress, and, sensing that the Maltz affair could prove politically damaging to the electoral chances of John F. Kennedy, from the Kennedy camp as well. Sinatra withstood the pressure for three weeks, then capitulated and fired Maltz, abandoning the film at the same time.

When he was elected, Kennedy gave Sinatra his most prestigious assignment ever, the task of hosting and organising the Inaugural Gala. This was not only to celebrate the Kennedy win but also to help recoup the depleted coffers of the Democratic Party, who had been left with a $4,000,000 debt incurred during the election campaign. The Gala, held in Washington's National Guard Armoury, raised the staggering sum of $1,500,000. Sinatra's debut as an impressario was impressive, with a cast that included Leonard Bernstein, Gene Kelly (who had flown in from Switzerland), Bette Davis, Ella Fitzgerald (who had come all the way from Australia), Ethel Merman, Laurence Olivier, Nat 'King' Cole, Jimmy Durante, Harry Belafonte, and Juliet Prowse. Kennedy spoke at the Gala to acknowledge his contribution: 'We're all indebted to a great friend, Frank Sinatra. Long before he could sing, he was pulling votes in a New Jersey precinct.' He added, 'Tonight we saw excellence', a phrase later used in trade-

paper advertising to commemorate the Gala

The next morning, after taking his Oath of Office, the President briefly attended a private party being given by Sinatra in his hotel suite. In retrospect, that visit and the Gala turned out to be the apogee of their friendship—in public at least. The beginning of the deterioration of Sinatra's long-standing support for the Democrats dates from this point, and, by the end of the Sixties, he had changed his political allegiances and become a vigorous campaigner for the Republican Party. The once fervent campaigner for Franklin Delano Roosevelt and his New Deal in the Forties was to become the supporter of Richard Nixon and Spiro Agnew

♪WHEN NO ONE CARES♪

Certainly media hostility to Sinatra's support of John F. Kennedy, which they saw as injecting an unwanted element of show business into politics, helped to create the rift between Sinatra and the Kennedy Clan. More important, however, was the attitude of Bobby Kennedy. He had thought – wrongly as it turned out – that Sinatra's alleged links with organised crime would prove an electoral liability. Nonetheless, he disapproved of his brother's association with Sinatra, recognising perhaps that, despite his position, John F. Kennedy was very much a star-struck man who relished the company and ambience of show-business personalities.

One of the other myths that has accumulated around Sinatra is that he was in some way responsible for the introduction of Marilyn Monroe to President John F. Kennedy, whose mistress she allegedly became. Certainly Monroe was a friend of Sinatra's and there is some evidence to show that she used her friendship with Sinatra to get close to the Clan and thus, perhaps through Peter Lawford, she may have got to meet John F. Kennedy. What is certain is that Monroe felt that Sinatra was one of the few men in her life she could trust, being quoted as having said shortly before her death, 'Frank has always been so kind and understanding. When I'm with him I feel I don't have to take pills or see a psychiatrist or anything else. He makes me feel secure and happy. He makes me laugh. I think he is the only man who has taught me how to love life. And he's really a gentle-

man.' With Sinatra, friendship was total.

By 1962, Bobby's disapproval of Sinatra and his friends had been demonstrated in a highly humiliating way to the entertainer. It had been announced by Sinatra that President Kennedy was going to be his guest at his house on Frank Sinatra Drive at Palm Springs. Sinatra had even begun the building of special facilities to house Kennedy and his entourage when, in March, it was announced that the President would be staying instead with Bing Crosby at *his* home near Palm Springs. The public explanation was that given by the Secret Service,

New Directions. Sinatra stages the Inaugural Gala for President Kennedy, routing out an impressive line-up of talent (*left*): from left to right, Nat King Cole, Harry Belafonte, Kay Thompson, Jimmy Durante, Helen Traubel, Sammy Cahn, Sidney Poitier (behind an unknown man), Gene Kelly, Janet Leigh, Peter Lawford, and Milton Berle. Democratic buddies, President John F. Kennedy and Sinatra at the Inaugural Ball on 20 January, 1961 (*above*)

119

who claimed that Crosby's home was easier to make secure. What appears to have happened is that Bobby Kennedy had finally managed to convince his brother of the undesirability of continued association with Sinatra.

The following year was a worse one for Sinatra, however. When he became Attorney General, Bobby Kennedy, who believed he knew the workings and ramifications of organised crime and had written a book, *The Enemy Within*, on the subject, instituted a purge on the gangsters, galvanising the hitherto dismissive FBI into action. One of their first activities was to put a number of key underworld figures under surveillance. One of these was Sam Giancana, who was also on a list put out in 1960 by the Nevada Gambling Control Board of those banned from entering any state gambling establishment. In 1962, Sinatra had opened his Cal-Neva Lodge, a hotel-cum-casino on the borders of California and Nevada with the state line actually running through the hotel. In July 1963, agents of the Gambling Control Board reported that Sam Giancana, still under surveillance, had spent some time at one of the Cal-Neva's chalets.

The Control Board formally issued charges against Sinatra as the owner of the Cal-Neva, stating that Giancana was known '. . . to have been entertained, harboured, and permitted to remain at Cal-Neva Lodge and to receive services and courtesies from the licensee, its representatives, employees, agents and directors.' At stake was Sinatra's licence to operate his casinos at the Cal-Neva and Las Vegas's Sands Hotel, in which he had a share.

At first, despite the publicity, Sinatra said that he would fight the Board. He had fifteen days in which to reply. Surprisingly, as the deadline approached, Sinatra decided not to oppose the Board's action and did not offer a defence. Instead, he issued a statement which read in part, 'Since I have decided that I belong in the entertainment industry and not in the gaming industry, no useful purpose would be served by devoting my time and energies convincing the Nevada gaming officials that I should be a part of their gaming industry. I have recently become associated with a major company in the entertainment industry (Warner Brothers) and in forming that association I have agreed to devote my full time and efforts to that company's activities in the entertainment industry.

'Accordingly, I have instructed my attorney to notify the Nevada gaming officials that I am withdrawing from the gaming industry in Nevada. . . .'

Not only was the publicity bad, Sinatra suffered financially too when he was forced to sell off assets valued at some $3,500,000.

Despite his breach with the Kennedy clan, Sinatra was deeply upset by the news of the President's assassination on 22 November, 1963, while he was working on the movie *Robin and the Seven Hoods*. Typical of the man whose 1945 film *The House I Live In* had been about intolerance, he made a speech to the cast and crew of the movie pleading with them not to generalise about Texans simply because

President Kennedy had been killed in Dallas.

He was still depressed when, on 8 December, 1963, Sinatra heard that his son, Frank Sinatra Jr, had been kidnapped from his room at Harrah's Lake Tahoe Casino, where he was singing with the newly re-formed Tommy Dorsey band. Sinatra had to wait out a terrifying twenty-four hours before the kidnappers contacted him to demand their ransom–$240,000– and give detailed instructions on how it was to be delivered. Three days later, Frank Jr was found wandering at 3.00 a.m. in Hollywood's Bel Air district.

For once the majority of the press were sympathetic towards Sinatra, except for the few that insisted the whole affair had been a publicity stunt. It hadn't. The FBI and the police had been brought in from the very beginning, the amateur kidnappers were caught within a matter of days of their victim's release, and most of the ransom money was recovered. After the trial, at which Sinatra father and son both had to undergo the defence's allegations of engineering a publicity stunt, the kidnappers were sentenced to long terms of imprisonment. Sinatra was quoted as saying, 'I used to worry constantly about some nuts kidnapping my kids, but I haven't thought about it for years, because the kids are all grown up.'

♫TAKING A CHANCE ON LOVE♪

After his divorce from Ava, Sinatra lived the life of a hedonistic Hollywood bachelor, with some of his romances being well publicised whereas others were rather less obviously in the public eye. It had taken him time totally to recover from the emotional trauma of his break-up with Ava: things looked rather more serious romantically, however, when in 1959 he met Juliet Prowse, a long-legged South African dancer brought in to replace Barrie Chase who had walked off the set of the movie *Can-Can* after disagreements about the number of

below Two giants of music come together to produce some of the singer's most interesting songs – Sinatra and Count Basie

opposite Sinatra, in a photograph shot by Robin Douglas-Home, one-time Sinatra hagiographer, takes time out for a reviving cup of tea at fifty

lances she was going to have compared with Shirley MacLaine. The star of *Can-Can*, Frank Sinatra was soon fascinated by Juliet, particularly as she showed herself to be self-possessed and totally professional in her attitude towards her career. After *Can-Can* was completed, Sinatra and Juliet were frequent companions, at movie premieres, recording sessions, and other similarly public places. She also displayed an enviable ability not to be rattled by the press, who naturally were deeply interested in the new woman in Sinatra's life. Not that, Sinatra being Sinatra, she was the only woman: during 1961, while still dating Juliet, Sinatra

was also to be seen in the company of other women, most notably actress Dorothy Provine, with whom he travelled around the Far East during Christmas 1961.

Then, with a suddenness that surprised even the media, Sinatra's engagement to Juliet Prowse was announced on 9 January, 1962. Juliet left for South Africa to see her parents, announcing, 'He doesn't want me to work. But I do, after working this long and hard for a career, I hate to give it up.' She didn't. On 22 January, 1962, the engagement was over, with an announcement from one of Sinatra's companies which read, 'Juliet Prowse and Frank

Sinatra today disclosed that they have called off their wedding plans. The pair in a joint statement said: "A conflict in career interests led us to make this decision. We both felt it wiser to make this move now rather than later." ' Certainly, after the experience of being 'Mr Gardner', it was unlikely that Sinatra would again marry a woman who was intent upon having her own career, even if his was very much in the ascendant.

Throughout the Sixties and until his 'retirement' in 1971, Sinatra continued to record for Reprise, experimenting with styles in order to keep up with changing audience tastes while at the same time not completely abandoning the essential qualities which accounted for his unique success. 1962 saw him making his first foray into jazz and moving away from the smoother arrangements of the Forties and Fifties with the album *Sinatra-Basie*. 'I've waited twenty years for this,' he was quoted as saying when he met Basie, and the resulting album, arranged by Neal Hefti, made the wait well worth while.

It was released in 1963, the year which saw Sinatra reunited on record with Nelson Riddle, for the first time since he had left Capitol Records to found Reprise. Riddle's contract with Capitol had finally ended. The result of their renewed collaboration was *The Concert Sinatra* and *Sinatra's Sinatra*; both were good but, in the final analysis, less exciting than might have been expected. They were technically superb, of course, but both albums somehow missed the inner life that had been an essential part of their previous successes. In 1964, Sinatra made his second LP with Count Basie, *It Might As Well Be Swing*. This time the orchestrations were by Quincy Jones and the album lacked the appeal of the first Sinatra-Basie LP.

1965 was a very good year for Sinatra in nearly every way, but in particular in his recording career. He won a Grammy (the recording industry's equivalent of the cinema's Oscar) for his disc 'It Was a Very Good Year', for the Best Male Vocal Performance, while his arranger-conductor Gordon Jenkins picked up his own Grammy for his work on the record. And Sinatra's autobiographical LP, *September of My Years*, also arranged and conducted by Jenkins, won another Grammy, as Album of the Year. There were, of course, many more Sinatra LPs and singles to come, but *September of My Years* is probably the finest and most moving album of his Reprise years. The numbers were filled with a lyrical romanticism as well as an often nakedly vulnerable emotionalism as Sinatra sang a portrait of a man not only reviewing his past from the standpoint of his fiftieth year but also coming to terms with his future.

As time went by, Sinatra was successfully to experiment with new arrangers and new orchestras, as well adapting his style and material to fit changing public tastes and, more importantly, to allow for the toll that age and use was inevitably taking on his voice. On record, Sinatra was able to control the sheer quality of his sound by his meticulous insistence on take after take until he was completely satisfied that what was on disc was exactly what he wanted to achieve. In concert and on television, his supreme showmanship, his by now mythical status as an entertainer, and, above all, his unique way with lyrics, managed to maintain the illusion of the singer still unmatched and inimitable, although the voice on its own was no longer the fine musical instrument it had been in his younger days.

Not that it mattered: on disc or in person, Sinatra was Sinatra and that was sufficient in itself, creating an ambience that was uniquely his, no matter what he did or sang. Actress and

jazz singer Annie Ross superbly summed up this special quality when she said, 'Sinatra reads a lyric so beautifully, and the way he phrases a song is better than ever it was, so much so that he doesn't really have to actually *sing*. He's also well aware of the kind of atmosphere, the kind of mood he creates; he makes you feel as if you personally are the one he's singing to.'

'**H**is singing is just terrific. He has this lovely warmth because he is a sad man. But, above all, it's his eyes I love. All his quiet charm comes from the eyes.'

JACQUELINE BISSET

That verdict, delivered in 1977, exactly sums up the essential appeal of Sinatra's singing. When he sings, he becomes the ultimate romantic, able with his voice to make love to each woman in his audience, matron or bobbysoxer, in so intimate a manner as to convince her that she alone is the object of his attentions. There are other singers who can lay claim to greater technical expertise. In the final judgement, that proves not to be enough. What they lack, and what makes Sinatra unique throughout his career, is the sexual empathy with the audience, live or on record, that made him a star.

The subsequent years were to see Sinatra make albums and singles with a fascinating variety of collaborators, including Don Costa, Duke Ellington, Morris Stoloff, Quincy Jones and Count Basie, and Gordon Jenkins. On 11 April, 1966, he recorded the theme song by Bert Kampfaert from an otherwise totally undistinguished movie, *A Man Could Get Killed*: the resulting single, 'Strangers in the Night', topped the charts in America as well as in many other countries, including Great Britain. He experimented with the Bossa Nova in a fascinating album *Francis Albert Sinatra and Antonio*

Carlos Jobim in 1967, adding an impressive mastery of Latin-American rhythms to his repertoire in the process, and in the same year he achieved his one and only gold disc for a single – in the duet 'Somethin' Stupid' which he made with his daughter Nancy. (Sinatra has made something of a running joke about the fact that even Grace Kelly received a gold disc for her duet 'True Love' with Bing Crosby in the 1956 movie *High Society*: one wonders how much genuine regret lies behind the banter.)

If Sinatra managed to achieve only one (shared) gold disc for his singles, his gold albums present a highly impressive list, all of them concentrated into the decade 1961 to 1970. Each represents the sale of records or tapes to the value of $1,000,000. In 1961, there was *Come Dance With Me*; there were four in 1962, *Frank Sinatra Sings Only For The Lonely*, *This Is Sinatra*, *Songs For Swingin' Lovers* and *Nice 'n' Easy*. In 1965 came *Sinatra's Sinatra*, his first gold album for Reprise; in 1966 three more, *Sinatra: A Man and His Music*, *September of My Years*, and *Strangers in the Night*; with two more in 1967, *That's Life* and *Sinatra at The Sands With Count Basie*, recorded at the Las Vegas hotel. In 1969, the year Sinatra went 'pop' with the single 'Cycles' (and also recorded his seminal number 'My Way'), the album *Cycles* earned a gold too. Finally, in 1970, there were a couple more gold albums, appropriately *Frank Sinatra's Greatest Hits* and *My Way*. (As a footnote to Sinatra's singing career, it is worth noting that he is credited as a co-writer of seven songs, 'I'm a Fool To Want You', 'Mistletoe and Holly', 'Mr Success', 'Peachtree Street', 'Sheila', 'Take My Love', and 'This Love of Mine'.)

By 1975, however, Sinatra was no longer making singles or albums that sold well or made the charts, hardly strange considering that he was now in his sixtieth year. Even such

Father Figure. Sinatra watches Frank Jr with the Dorsey Orchestra on television in the mid Sixties (*below*) and shows parental appreciation of his son (who sensibly wears a Reprise badge on his jacket) while his first wife Nancy looks on approvingly (*opposite, above left*). With his younger daughter Tina (*opposite, above right*), Sinatra attends a party in Las Vegas in 1969, and elder sister Nancy (*opposite, below*) and father bridge the generation gap and record together, although Nancy breaks up during the session, leaving the unflappable Sinatra to sing on alone

offerings as 'Send In the Clowns' from the Steven Sondheim musical *A Little Night Music*, a number relying almost completely upon its lyric for its greatest effect, failed to meet with success. The truth was that, on disc at any rate, it was now time for Sinatra gracefully to fade away, leaving his singing to live performances where the songs could be carried by the sheer charisma of his presence.

Throughout the Sixties, Sinatra kept up a steady schedule of concerts and nightclub work, the most memorable being his 1965 debut at the famous 4 July Newport Jazz Festival, where he was accompanied by the Count Basie Orchestra. Typically for the man who was used to travelling between engagements in his private Lear jet, Sinatra descended upon New-

port by helicopter, sang, and rose again into the sky, adding another dimension to his legend. What he sang may not have been jazz but it was what the crowds wanted and Sinatra departed to an ovation, leaving *Variety* to describe the 1965 Newport Jazz Festival as 'Sinatra's Festival'. Sinatra immediately followed this with an eight-concert record-breaking tour with Basie.

1965 also marked the first transmission of his television show, the spectacular *Frank Sinatra: A Man and His Music*, a one-man songfest that finally conquered the electronic medium for Sinatra. Sponsored by Budweiser Beer, and transmitted by NBC on 24 November, the show featured a relaxed and on-form Sinatra singing seventeen standards and a

Young at Heart. Sinatra meets Mia Farrow on the set of *Von Ryan's Express* at Twentieth Century-Fox studios (*right*), and their engagement–he is fifty, she is twenty-one–is announced while they cruise on the yacht *Southern Breeze* (*below*)

highly appropriate new song, 'It Was A Very Good Year'. The show was an immense success. The critics loved it: there was even a glowing review from the critic of the Hearst newspaper chain, a group previously noted for their implacable hatred of the entertainer, in which the show was called 'The class–and the best musical TV hour of the year . . . A shining hour on the tube'. The special also won the coveted Peabody and Edison Awards as well as several Emmies. It was later to be repeated by public demand. Sinatra had licked the one remaining major entertainment medium–television.

♪THE SEPTEMBER OF MY YEARS♪

Finally, on 12 December, 1965, Sinatra celebrated his fiftieth birthday with a party thrown for him by his ex-wife Nancy at the Beverly Wilshire Hotel in Hollywood. That Sunday evening was marked by the sort of celebration that could only take place in Hollywood: Milton Berle was the master of ceremonies, Jack Haley Jr, later to produce the large-scale compilation movie *That's Entertainment*, put on a witty collection of scenes from Sinatra's films, and inevitably, given the occasion and

The third Mrs Sinatra in Hollywood (*left*), and she and her husband have a quiet word during a break in a recording session at Hollywood's Sunset Boulevard studios (*below*)

the celebrants, Sammy Davis Jr burst out of a cake and sang a parody of a song from *Robin and the Seven Hoods*, a little number entitled 'My Kind of Man, Sinatra Is'. Clearly *Never So Few* was completely forgotten.

Notable by her absence was Mia Farrow, Sinatra's new love interest. Mia, the daughter of Australian-born Hollywood movie director John Farrow and Maureen O'Sullivan, one-time Jane to Johnny Weissmuller's Tarzan, was providing the media with their latest source material for Sinatra-baiting headlines. On this occasion, Sinatra appears to have led with his chin, since there was a thirty-year gap in their ages.

They had first met in October 1964 on the set of *Von Ryan's Express*, then being completed at the Twentieth Century-Fox studios. The popular soap-opera *Peyton Place*, in which Mia starred as Allison MacKenzie, was also filmed on the Fox lot. At first shy with Sinatra, Mia soon began to see him in private. Then the journalists got wind of the liaison: the couple made their first public appearance in April 1965

at a charity lunch in Hollywood. The affair was perfect for media coverage and the media took full advantage of the fact. Maureen O'Sullivan commented on being asked about a possible marriage between the two, 'Marry Mia? It would make better sense if he married me.' The pairing of Sinatra and Mia made even better material for nightclub comics.

In August of 1965, pursued by press comment, Sinatra chartered a 168-foot yacht, *Southern Breeze*, and with Rosalind Russell and her husband Frederick Brisson, William and Edie Goetz, and Claudette Colbert and her husband

Dr Joel Pressman as 'chaperones' for him and
Mia, they set sail for a four-week cruise out of
Newport, Rhode Island. The media kept the
cruise under observation, claiming to their
delight that the *Southern Breeze* had been
visited off Hyannis Port, Massachusetts, by
Jacqueline Kennedy, the widow of the late
President John F. Kennedy. In fact, Sinatra had
gone to visit her father-in-law Joseph Kennedy
ashore, but the press had a field day with the
story, until Jackie Kennedy was forced to issue
a denial that she had ever gone aboard the
yacht.

There was still more adverse publicity to
come from the cruise: a crewman, travelling
back to the *Southern Breeze* with another crew
member and two women, was drowned when
their dinghy capsized. The tragedy had nothing
to do with Sinatra, since the dead crewman was
the responsibility of the chartered vessel's
captain. Nonetheless, the press excoriated
Sinatra, managing to make the incident appear
his fault. The rest of the cruise was cancelled as,
once again, Sinatra found his love life in the
public domain.

After the party at the Beverly Wilshire,
Sinatra had gone on to make a birthday visit to
Mia, to be greeted with her 'present': she had
had her hair cut to the boyish style then being
affected by Liza Minnelli. More press speculation, on the lines that she had done it in order to
draw attention to her failure to be invited to the
hotel birthday party, inevitably followed. The
most sensible reaction came from Twentieth
Century-Fox, who arranged for Allison Mac-
Kenzie of *Peyton Place* to have her locks shorn
to match Mia's latest hair style!

♪LET ME TRY AGAIN♫

On 19 July, 1966, Sinatra and Mia were married
in Las Vegas in the suite of the Sands Hotel's
manager, Jack Entratter, the best man being
movie producer William Goetz, one-time
'chaperone' for the ill-fated cruise of the

Who wants to be a millionaire?
Sinatra lifts off from Warner
Brothers studios in one of his two
helicopters (*below*), en route for his
home in Palm Springs, and reads a
script at home in a living room
furnished with $5,000 worth of hi fi
equipment and Ringo, his
Australian sheepdog (*right*)

Southern Breeze. The couple entered marriage with the firm intention of trying to ensure that their careers did not conflict in any way. Sinatra was also determined that their age difference should not affect them and tried hard to fit his plans in with those of his new wife. He was apparently happy to sit in the din of a discotheque while his wife danced the frug with her friends Roddy McDowell, Jack Haley Jr, or writer Leonard Gershe.

Mia spent the spring of 1967 filming *A Dandy in Aspic* in Europe with Laurence Harvey, her first major starring role, after having accompanied Sinatra there while he made *The Naked Runner*. It was clear even after the first few months that their marriage was far from well: the difference in their ages was beginning to impose inevitable strains. Nevertheless, Mia agreed to make *The Detective* with Sinatra after *A Dandy in Aspic* was completed.

Before that, however, Sinatra garnered a few more headlines from an incident in the Sands Hotel in Las Vegas. There was a brawl involving the entertainer after his gambling credit had been cut off by the hotel. The upshot was that Sinatra severed his exclusive contract with the Sands, switching instead to the rival Caesar's Palace, and it was the end of his long friendship with Jack Entratter.

By the time, in October 1967, Sinatra was

left Come Fly With Me: Sinatra's private Gulfstream jet, pale yellow and upholstered in leather, with a padded toilet and a blonde stewardess named Hannelori Kauspe brings the entertainer to Britain in 1970

below Still in the swim at fifty

ready for his wife to report for filming of *The Detective*, a major new rift had opened between them. Mia had been offered the lead in Paramount's film version of Ira Levin's best-seller, *Rosemary's Baby*: her role in *The Detective* only amounting to a co-starring part, Mia chose to start filming on *Rosemary's Baby* under the direction of Roman Polanski. William Castle, producer on the Polanski film, was quoted as saying that Sinatra had given Mia an ultimatum: either she abandoned *Rosemary's Baby* or he would divorce her. Mia chose to complete the movie while English actress Jacqueline Bisset replaced her in *The Detective*.

On 22 November, 1967, an announcement was made that Sinatra and Mia had 'mutually agreed to a trial separation'. That separation, despite an abortive attempt at a reconciliation during a Christmas 'truce', proved to be a permanent one. In January 1968, Mia joined Beatles John Lennon and George Harrison in India for meditation with the then fashionable pop stars' guru, the improbable Maharishi Mahesh Yogi. Ostensibly Mia had gone East to open up her mind in the company of others of her own generation. The experience did nothing for her relationship with Sinatra and, just over two years from the date of their marriage, on 15 August, 1968, Sinatra and Mia were divorced in Mexico.

The Sixties ended painfully for Sinatra when, on 25 January, 1969, his father Anthony Martin Sinatra died at the age of seventy-four in a Houston hospital. In January 1970, the groundbreaking ceremony for the 'Anthony Martin Sinatra Hospital' took place in Palm Springs: the following year Sinatra, who had donated $800,000 towards the building, dedicated the hospital and was awarded an honorary medical degree. His mother was present at the ceremony, as was Vice-President Spiro Agnew and Governor Ronald Reagan, and the day was named Frank Sinatra Day by the mayor of Palm Springs, Howard Wiffe.

Sinatra himself entered hospital in 1970 for surgery to correct a contraction of his hand which caused him great pain and made it impossible for him fully to open the affected hand. The operation forced him to drop out of a movie he was scheduled to make for Warner Brothers, *Dead Right*.

'Sinatra never seemed to be alone. There were always four men with him; fellows who never take their hats off, even in night clubs. It's all a bit like a gangster film.'

TREVOR HOWARD

The previous year had seen another attempt to link him with organised crime when the New Jersey Crime Commission subpoenaed Sinatra as he came ashore from his yacht to have dinner at a New Jersey restuarant. They wanted him to testify on the attempts of organised crime syndicates to infiltrate 'legitimate' businesses. Later it transpired that the Commission had full knowledge from FBI and other sources that Sinatra would be able to tell them nothing of value. Nevertheless, they pressed ahead in an attempt to force Sinatra to testify in public. He refused and his attorneys appealed to the United States Appeals Court, which upheld the Committee. The legal battle went all the way to the Federal Supreme Court, where a contempt charge was upheld against Sinatra. He finally appeared before the Committee, testifying for an hour. All charges were dropped and it later turned out, according to an off-the-record statement by a Committee member, that Sinatra had been singled out because of his name and the concomitant publicity it would bring to the investigation.

Politics had been one of the factors which had led to the breakdown of Sinatra's marriage to Mia: in 1968, Mia supported Bobby Kennedy for the Democratic nomination, whereas Sinatra, with his understandable dislike for the Attorney General, was all for Senator Hubert Humphrey. When Bobby was assassinated

SINATRA 'A MAN WHO IS ABOVE THE LAW'

Singer in Mafia investigation

Sinatra is questioned on Mafia

From Our Own Correspondent

New York, Feb. 18

Frank Sinatra, the singer, appeared unexpectedly last night before a hurriedly convened session of the New Jersey commission investigating organized crime in the state.

...lasting about 90...

...tra was ...k Court ...h filthy ...above

...le by ...New ...nittee ...links.
...the

singer, said: "If anybody can come before this court with more filthy hands, it is beyond me."

The commission has subpoenaed Sinatra to find out what he knows about organised crime in New Jersey. Phelan claimed the subpoena arose from a visit by Sinatra to a restaurant

frequented by Simone (Sam the Plumber) de Cavalante, who has been charged with a part in running a vast illegal Mafia lottery.

The investigation into New Jersey's Mafia "family," suspected of milking more than a billion dollars a year from the state, was sparked off by a voice from the grave.

Louis Saperstein was said to have left a note to his family with detailed information for the authorities—just in case he died.

Saperstein, a suspected Mafia victim, died after drinking enough arsenic "to kill a mule" which was concealed in his drink. Italian pastry

BEAR by Posy

Would you be an angel?

below Man in the spotlight. Sinatra sings goodbye at his 'farewell' concert at the Los Angeles Music Center on 14 June, 1971

right Having switched political sides and become a robust Republican, rumour has it (wrongly) that Sinatra might follow his one-time co-star George Murphy into senatorial politics. From the London *Sun* on 30 April, 1971

Sinatra is 'aiming for the Senate'

FROM RAY KERRISON

NEW YORK, Thursday. —Frank Sinatra, who recently retired from showbusiness, will soon announce his candidacy for the United States Senate.

That, at least, is the loudest, hottest rumour in Hollywood, according to the film capital's best-informed gossip columnist, Joyce Haber.

Reason

Miss Haber, of the Los Angeles Times, says there

ing out with the late Bobby Kennedy he threw his support to California's Republican Governor, former film star Ronald Reagan.

The new rumours, however, conflict directly with Sinatra's own showbusiness farewell statement.

while in Los Angeles on 5 June, 1968, the Humphrey camp turned out to be as nervous of Sinatra's support as Bobby Kennedy had been. This brush-off finally finished Sinatra's association with the Democrats. In 1971 he was as staunchly behind the Republican Party as he had ever been in support of their rivals.

But first, he retired. The retirement was, however, only in his capacity as a professional entertainer. Sinatra still remained a highly active businessman. Nevertheless, in March 1971, he announced that: 'For over three decades I have had the great and good fortune to enjoy a rich, rewarding and deeply satisfying career as a public figure. Those years, fruitful, busy, uptight, loose, sometimes boisterous, occasionally sad but always exciting, allowed me little opportunity for reflection, reading, self-examination and the need every thinking man has for a fallow period.'

Being Sinatra, he retired not with a statement but with an occasion, a gala evening held in the Los Angeles Music Centre on 14 June, 1971. In actual fact it had been announced as a concert for the Motion Picture and Television Relief Fund. Instead, it became Sinatra's farewell concert, complete with Bob Hope, Cary Grant, Jack Benny, Rosalind Russell, and the egregious David Frost. Sinatra talked and sang, received ovation after ovation, and heard Rosalind Russell say, '... it's time to put back the Kleenex and stifle the sob, for we still have the man, we still have the blue eyes, those wonderful blue eyes, that smile, for the last time we have the man, the greatest entertainer of the twentieth century.'

right Lucille Ball is greeted by Sinatra at the 1973 Gala Friars Club Testimonial for Milton Berle

below No mean golfer himself, Sinatra sponsored the first Frank Sinatra Invitation Golf Tournament in Palm Springs, attracting international pros and amateurs

♪CHANGE PARTNERS♫

Immediately he began to campaign for Ronald Reagan, becoming co-chairman of the committee for his re-election as Governor of California. Reagan won.

In the autumn of 1972, Sinatra turned his

attention to the campaign for Richard Nixon and Spiro Agnew. Sinatra, the politician, was in his element once more as he sang new lyrics, written by Sammy Cahn, to the tune of 'The Lady Is a Tramp': this time the words were a panegyric for Spiro Agnew, 'The Gentleman Is a Champ'. The admiration was mutual. In November 1972, a few days before the election, Sinatra was awarded the Medallion of Valour by Baron Edmund de Rothschild for all his generosity towards the State of Israel. During a previous tour of Israel, all the funds raised by Sinatra had been turned over by him for an Arab-Israeli Youth Centre in Nazareth, and Sinatra had laid the foundation stone himself. And, on the evening he received the Medallion of Valour, Sinatra's presence brought about the pledging of some $6,500,000 for Israel. Said Spiro Agnew, 'A legend in his own time, not only in the world of entertainment, but in the world of philanthropy, a man who has unselfishly used his blessings, the blessings bestowed by a God-given talent and hard work, to benefit his fellow man.'

During his two and a half years of retirement, Sinatra gave only one concert. It was at the White House on 17 April, 1973, at a state dinner given for President Andreotti of Italy. The concert, with Sinatra accompanied by Nelson Riddle and including songs which ranged from 'The House I Live In' through 'Moonlight in Vermont' to 'I've Got The World on a String', brought him an ovation led by the two presidents. And he heard Nixon say, 'This house is honoured to have a man whose parents were

left Before his move to the political right, Sinatra and fellow Democrat Dean Martin pose with California's Republican Governor, Ronald Reagan, and supporters Bob Hope and John Wayne at a 1970 fund-raising rally

below Higher Society Than Ever! After singing at a White House Gala for President Andreotti of Italy (second left), Sinatra poses with President Nixon and Mrs Nixon (right), with Vice-President Spiro Agnew on the left, Mrs Agnew between Sinatra and Nixon, and Mrs Andreotti next to the entertainer

born in Italy, but yet from humble beginnings went to the very top in entertainment.' Emotionally, Sinatra ended the evening in tears.

He also ended his retirement. Possibly his appetite for applause had been whetted by the response of the White House audience or perhaps he was simply bored by the inactivity of 'retirement'. Whatever the reason, in June 1973, he recorded the album *Ol' Blue Eyes is Back* with Gordon Jenkins and Don Costa sharing the arranging and conducting honours. Appropriately, one of the tracks was 'Let Me Try Again'. And the magic was still there.

He also came back on television with a one-hour special on NBC, shown on 18 November, 1973. The publicity for the show was good and strong, the reviews enthusiastic, with two conductor-arrangers, Gordon Jenkins and Don Costa. Said television writer John J. O'Connor, 'Well, Ol' Blue Eyes did it. Frank Sinatra took an hour of television and turned it into the best popular-music special of the year.' Only the ratings were less encouraging. Sinatra had been beaten into third place, with the television audience making their second choice a Dinah Shore special and giving the lead to George C. Scott and Diana Rigg in the movie *Hospital.*

He made his first appearance 'live' in Las Vegas, at Caesar's Palace Hotel on 25 January, 1974, and in March was chosen by the American Film Institute to host their tribute to actor James Cagney. Then, keeping up the momentum of a comeback that was considerably more energetic than the complete careers of other singers, Sinatra embarked in April on a thirteen-concert, eight-city tour which proved that, given an audience, the old Sinatra magic could still be as potent as ever. He played nearly all the time to good audiences and most of the reviews were excellent.

There were dissenting voices as well, however, notably a savage attack by *Rolling Stone*'s Ralph J. Gleason in June 1974, who wrote, 'It is simply weird now to see him all glossed up like a wax dummy, with that rug on his head looking silly, and the onstage movement, which used to be panther-tense, is now a self-conscious hoodlum bustle. It's even odder to see him with the bodyguards and hear all the gossip about his coterie of friends and their capers in this club or that hotel or that gambling joint . . . there are those of us who still dig his voice . . . but for whom Ol' Blue Eyes is a drag that Frankie never was. . . .' *Rolling Stone* colleague, Paul Hendrickson, saw things differently, redressing

the balance: 'Somehow it all begins to work on me too. By the time the tour hits Chicago, the Voice is making me—yes—tingle. It is almost as if this haunting, beautiful voice coming at us from the stage has a life of its own.'

♪MY WAY♩

When Sinatra toured Australia in July 1974, he was to find that he was still as capable of feuding with the media as ever he had been. It began in Melbourne when he was constantly interrupted by photographers and journalists while setting up for a concert. The explosion finally came when Sinatra had to force his way onto the stage through a phalanx of jostling pressmen and a barrage of flashbulbs in order to give his concert. The performance was stopped and Sinatra attacked the Australian press: 'Ladies and gentlemen, the men who work for the press are bums and parasites who never do an honest day's work in their lives. And the women reporters generally are all hookers. And I hope I don't have to explain to you the word "hooker". But I'm not particular. I'd give them a dollar fifty.'

'**H**e could be terribly nice one minute . . . well, not so nice the next.'

PRINCE CHARLES

To put it mildly, the Australians did not take kindly to Sinatra's outburst. The debacle rapidly escalated so that there were hostilities on two separate fronts. There was, of course, the by now familiar sight of Sinatra locked in combat with the media, but this time there was an added element in that he found he had taken on the Australian trade unions as well. The Transport Workers Union announced that it would ban its members from fuelling Sinatra's

private aircraft, and it was also reported that union members had refused to serve Sinatra and his entourage with food and drink in their suites at Melbourne's Southern Cross Hotel.

Hostilities reached such an absurd level that finally Bob Hawke, President of the Australian Labour Party and also head of the Australian Council of Trade Unions, flew to Sydney from Melbourne to meet with Sinatra's lawyer, Milton A. Rudio, in order to thrash out a peace settlement that would save the threatened tour. Adding an extra dimension to an already somewhat ludicrous situation, in the best tradition of top-level negotiations, a joint face-saving statement was issued from the two camps after discussions lasting four hours. It read, in part: 'Frank Sinatra did not intend any general reflection on the moral character of the working members of the Australian media. He, of course, reserves the right to comment on the quality of the professional performances of those working members of the media who he believes are subject to criticism on professional grounds, just as he acknowledges their right in this respect to his professional performance. . . . The unions recognise the unique international status of Frank Sinatra and his understandable desire to be protected from an uninhibited exposure to the media. . . .'

Peace was restored. Sinatra was not just a man, a star, or even a superstar—he was the possessor of 'unique international status'! The concerts he had threatened to cancel were reinstated, and Sinatra threw in a free television show for good measure. But while the furore raged in the media, it became transparently clear that the Sinatra who had come out of retirement was unchanged. He was nearly sixty, his legendary position in the history of show business was totally assured, and yet, deep down inside him, he still carried the terrible and uncontrollable urge unneces-

sarily to demonstrate his power in battles with the media. It is difficult to imagine what his companion on the tour, Barbara Marx, must have made of the whole business. Clearly, however, it did not adversely affect her relationship with Sinatra.

1974 also saw Sinatra make a brief cameo screen comeback, as one of the presenter-narrators of MGM's superb musical compilation *That's Entertainment*, sharing the task with Fred Astaire, Gene Kelly, Elizabeth Taylor, James Stewart, Bing Crosby, Liza Minnelli, Donald O'Connor, Debbie Reynolds, and Mickey Rooney. It was a somewhat unnerving experience to be able to compare the fifty-nine year-old Sinatra, with his unlikely-looking hair and thickened waist, with the youthful, lithe and undernourished figure of his early MGM days.

There was more trouble for Sinatra in September when he appeared with Frank Sinatra Jr and Nancy Jr at Harrah's Lake Tahoe (where Frank Jr had been kidnapped in 1963). Said *Variety*: '. . . [the show] was marred by some hisses, catcalls and boos as Sinatra again lambasted the press, this time apologising to hookers for comparing them to newswomen, and calling the press "a bunch of goddam liars".' Once more Sinatra was proving that the self-destructive side of his nature was still, given the appropriate stimuli, as vigorous as ever: this review must rate among his worst. The year ended with Sinatra repeating history by regaining the Hollywood Women's Press Club Sour Apple Award, for least cooperation, an award revived specially to give to Sinatra.

1975 was better. He appeared at Caesar's Palace in March, moving on to Canada for concerts at the Maple Leaf Garden in Toronto. Then he began his first European tour since 1962, arriving in London on 14 May, 1975, with Barbara Marx. The then British Prime

145

this page Sinatra comes back with a bang, wowing them out East, in Tokyo in July 1974 (*right*), and filling New York's Uris Theater in September 1975 and (*below*) escorting Jacqueline Onassis after the show

opposite End of a Line. Sinatra with Dolly and his long-time friend and some-time bodyguard and restaurateur, Jilly Rizzo (*above*). In January 1977, a grieving Sinatra and his fourth wife Barbara leave St Louis Catholic Church in Cathedral City, California, after a service for Dolly, killed in an air crash earlier that month (*below*)

Minister, Harold Wilson, a man with a keen eye for personal publicity, took advantage of the visit and invited Sinatra to his residence, 10 Downing Street, where Sinatra and Barbara spent some twenty minutes talking with Wilson and, somewhat incongruously, the Prime Minister of Fiji.

Sinatra's European tour took him to the Sporting Club in Monte Carlo on 19 May, the Palais de Congres in Paris on the following day, Vienna on 22 May, Munich the next day, and Frankfurt on 25 May. In Germany Sinatra received rough handling from the media, who raked up all the old stories for news readers. Additionally, the concerts were poorly attended: the Hamburg concert was cancelled because of poor advance sales and Sinatra himself took Berlin out of the schedule for the same

reason. His two concerts at London's Albert Hall on 29 and 30 May were well received, by fans and critics alike, and he played to full houses, going on record as saying that he would never forget the reception given him by the British fans. He proved this sentiment by returning to play the London Palladium for a week in November 1975.

Before that, however, he had returned to America where he appeared on Broadway for two weeks with Count Basie and Ella Fitzgerald at the Uris Theatre in September. The engagement was a triumphant reaffirmation of the success of his comeback. In those two weeks the show grossed an incredible record of $1,088,000. He even managed to top this by appearing on a Jerry Lewis telethon in aid of muscular dystrophy: not only did his appear-

ance help raise huge sums of money from the viewers but Sinatra paid his thirty musicians himself and gave $25,000 to the fund in the name of his grand-daughter, Angela Jennifer.

In 1976 he married Barbara Marx, the former wife of screen comedian Zeppo Marx, at the Palm Springs home of Walter P. Annenberg, on 12 July. His loyalty, a trait that has perhaps been one of the strongest in his life and career, was marked by the fact that disgraced ex-Vice-President Spiro T. Agnew, once a regular Sinatra house-guest at his Palm Springs home, attended the wedding, along with some one hundred and thirty others.

While flying from Palm Springs to Las Vegas to see Sinatra's performance at Caesar's Palace on 6 January, 1977, Dolly Sinatra died when the chartered aircraft crashed in California. On 2

below After a Sinatra-Robert Merrill concert at New York's Carnegie Hall in April 1977 in aid of medical charities, Sinatra watches Governor Hugh Carey carve up the cake that is New York State

opposite Sinatra, the first solo performer to fill London's Albert Hall for a week, swings into action in 1977 to a rapturous reception

N.Y. State Gov. CAREY

November, 1977, Sinatra gave a testimonial dinner in honour of his mother's memory in the Crown Room of Las Vegas's Stardust Hotel. The $500 plate dinner raised some one million dollars, and this was donated to Dolly Sinatra's favourite charity, the Villa Scalabrini of Los Angeles Retirement Center, with the money to be used for the construction of a chapel, kitchen and dining facilities. It was a fitting tribute to the woman who had had more influence than any other in Sinatra's life, the woman to whom he always brought his women friends for one of Dolly Sinatra's home-cooked Italian dinners, to gain her comments and approval.

In February to March 1977, he had added to

his legend by becoming the first solo artist to appear for a whole week at London's Albert Hall. And on 4 July, 1977, Frank Sinatra was awarded the Freedom of the City of Philadelphia, becoming only the fourth person to receive this honour, joining Herbert Hoover, Harry S. Truman, and Bob Hope.

Throughout his career, Sinatra had been constantly dogged by tales of his alleged associations with gangsters and figures from the world of organised crime. It is fascinating to see, therefore, the role he chose to make his acting comeback in the 1977 made-for-television movie *Contract on Cherry Street*. Sinatra, to quote from the publicity given out by Columbia Pictures Television, 'plays a New York City cop who goes underground to break up the syndicates'.

Contract on Cherry Street, which co-starred Martin Balsam and Verna Bloom, was first shown on NBC on 19 November, 1977. It was well received by *Variety*, who wrote of the movie itself, '*Contract on Cherry Street* is an involving and ofttimes gripping crime melodrama which establishes its sense of outrage and communicates its concerns with taut precision and much accumulated power. Frank Sinatra stars as a New York police inspector fed up with lax courts, liberal judges and socially articulate lawyers who provide a revolving door for habitual criminals. So, because of the system's inherent stopgaps, Sinatra and his squad spearhead their own brand of justice.' Of the star's performance, *Variety* said, 'Sinatra turns in a rewarding performance of much emotional muscle, lean, spare but strong . . .'.

It is claimed that Sinatra wanted to make *Contract on Cherry Street* because the book upon which it was based, by Phil Rosenberg, was his mother's favourite novel. No matter what the motivation behind Sinatra's return to acting, his performance augured well for the future of the superstar.

Budd Schulberg's famous novel *What Makes Sammy Run?* describes the rise and rise of a fictional show-business character from obscurity to fame. It is tempting to pose the same question about Sinatra. But it is patently obvious that there can be no empirical answer. Sinatra's nature is too complex, too often contradictory, its apparently irreconcilable elements fused into the personality of the man and the legend.

In short, Sinatra is Jekyll and he is also Hyde. He is both the shy kid determined to break out of Hoboken and become a star like his idol Bing Crosby *and* the brash superstar who reviles the media and calls a Washington newswoman 'nothing but a two dollar broad'. He is the man who gives—and demands—utter loyalty and he is also the man who never forgets a slight. He is capable of undertaking a gruelling three-month tour around the world to raise money for children's charities, paying the near million pound expenses himself: he is also capable of interrupting a concert to call newsmen 'bums

and parasites' and women reporters 'broads and buck-and-a-half hookers'. He can be foul mouthed and he can also seduce most women with the sexual intimacy of his singing.

In the ultimate analysis, only Sinatra himself can say what makes him run. The rest of us have to be content—and fortunate—to be the recipients of his immense talents as an entertainer. Long after the headlines, the battles, and the ephemeral myths that surround Sinatra have vanished, there will remain the hard, unalterable core of his work, on record and on film. That legacy is what the essential Frank Sinatra will come to mean—a unique voice that belongs to a unique legend.

below Love and Marriage. Sinatra and fourth wife Barbara in New York in 1977

opposite At sixty-one, Sinatra dons the Dodgers' uniform to pitch the first ball and start the game. He promises to sing at every season's opener if the Dodgers win the series. Things don't go exactly to plan, though: he forgets some of the lyrics of 'The Star Spangled Banner' and his voice breaks on a couple of notes. Still, Ol' Blue Eyes is back again, and in there pitching–*his* way!

Filmography

LAS VEGAS NIGHTS
Paramount 1941

Produced by William LeBaron. Directed by Ralph Murphy. Original screenplay by Ernest Pagano and Harry Clork. Musical director: Victor Young. Musical advisor: Arthur Franklin. Musical numbers staged by LeRoy Prinz. Running time: 89 minutes.

WITH Constance Moore, Bert Wheeler, Phil Regan, Lillian Cornell, Virginia Dale, Hank Ladd, and Tommy Dorsey and His Orchestra.
SINATRA sang with the Tommy Dorsey Orchestra as soloist.
HIS SONG: 'I'll Never Smile Again' by Ruth Lowe.

SHIP AHOY
Metro-Goldwyn-Mayer 1942

Produced by Jack Cummings. Directed by Edward Buzzell. Screenplay by Harry Clork. Music supervised and conducted by George Stoll. Running time: 95 minutes.

WITH Eleanor Powell, Red Skelton, Bert Lahr, Virginia O'Brien, and Tommy Dorsey and His Orchestra.
SINATRA sang with the Tommy Dorsey Orchestra and with the Pied Pipers.
HIS SONGS: 'The Last Call for Love' by Burton Lane, E. Y. Harburg, and Margery Cummings. 'Poor You' by Burton Lane and E. Y. Harburg.

REVEILLE WITH BEVERLY
Columbia 1943

Produced by Sam White. Directed by Charles Barton. Original screenplay by Howard J. Green, Jack Henley, and Albert Duffy. Musical director: Morris Stoloff. Running time: 78 minutes.

WITH Ann Miller, William Wright, Dick Purcell, and Franklin Pangborn.
SINATRA made a three-minute singing appearance.
HIS SONG: 'Night and Day' by Cole Porter.

HIGHER AND HIGHER
RKO 1943

Produced and directed by Tim Whelan. Screenplay by
Jay Dratler and Ralph Spence. Additional dialogue by
William Bowers and Howard Harris. Based on the play
by Gladys Hurlbut and Joshua Logan. Musical
director: Constantin Bakaleinikoff. Musical
arrangements for Frank Sinatra by Axel Stordahl.
Running time: 90 minutes.

WITH Michèle Morgan, Jack Haley, Leon Errol, Marcy
McGuire, Victor Borge, Mary Wickes, Barbara Hale,
Mel Torme, and Dooley Wilson.
SINATRA's first acting role: he played Frank, a well-to-
do suitor of a pseudo heiress.
HIS SONGS: 'You Belong in a Love Song', 'I Couldn't
Sleep a Wink Last Night', 'A Lovely Way to Spend an
Evening', 'The Music Stopped', and 'I Saw You First',
all by Jimmy McHugh and Harold Adamson.

STEP LIVELY
RKO 1944

Produced by Robert Fellows. Directed by Tim Whelan.
Screenplay by Warren Duff and Peter Milne. Based on
the play *Room Service* by John Murray and Allen
Boretz. Musical director: Constantin Bakaleinikoff.
Musical arrangements for Frank Sinatra by Axel
Stordahl. Musical numbers created and staged by Ernst
Matray. Running time: 88 minutes.

WITH George Murphy, Adolphe Menjou, Gloria
de Haven, Walter Slezak, Eugene Pallette, and Dorothy
Malone.
SINATRA played Glen–a country bumpkin–with dreams
of becoming a playwright.
HIS SONGS: 'Come Out, Come Out, Wherever You Are',
'Where Does Love Begin?', 'As Long as There's Music',
and 'Some Other Time', all by Jule Styne and
Sammy Cahn.

ANCHORS AWEIGH
Metro-Goldwyn-Mayer 1945
Technicolor

Produced by Joe Pasternak. Directed by George Sidney.
Screenplay by Isobel Lennart. Based on a story by
Natalie Marcin. Music supervised and conducted by
George Stoll. Frank Sinatra's vocal arrangements by
Axel Stordahl. Dance sequences created by Gene Kelly.
'Tom & Jerry' cartoon directed by Fred Quimby.
Running time: 143 minutes.

WITH Kathryn Grayson, Gene Kelly, Jose Iturbi, Dean
Stockwell, Pamela Britton, Rags Ragland, and Billy
Gilbert.
SINATRA played sailor Clarence Doolittle on shore leave
in Los Angeles–falling in love in the process.
HIS SONGS: 'We Hate to Leave', 'What Makes the
Sunset?', 'The Charm of You', 'I Begged Her', and 'I
Fall in Love Too Easily' by Jule Styne and Sammy
Cahn; 'Lullaby' (*'Wiegenlied'*) by Johannes Brahms.

153

THE HOUSE I LIVE IN
RKO 1945

Produced by Frank Ross. Directed by Mervyn LeRoy. Original screenplay by Albert Maltz. Musical director: Axel Stordahl. Incidental score by Roy Webb. Running time: 10 minutes.

SINATRA played himself straightening out children on the subject of racial and religious bigotry. (The film received a special Oscar.)
HIS SONGS: 'If You Are But a Dream' by Nathan J. Bonx, Jack Fulton, and Moe Jaffe (adapted from Anton Rubinstein's 'Romance'); 'The House I Live In' by Earl Robinson and Lewis Allan.

TILL THE CLOUDS ROLL BY
Metro-Goldwyn-Mayer 1946
Technicolor

Produced by Arthur Freed. Directed by Richard Whorf. Screenplay by Myles Connolly and Jean Holloway. Based on the life and music of Jerome Kern. Music supervised and conducted by Lennie Hayton. Musical numbers staged and directed by Robert Alton. Judy Garland's numbers directed by Vincente Minnelli. Running time: 137 minutes.

WITH June Allyson, Lucille Bremer, Judy Garland, Kathryn Grayson, Van Heflin, Lena Horne, Van Johnson, Angela Lansbury, Tony Martin, Virginia O'Brien, Dinah Shore, and Robert Walker.
SINATRA made a guest appearance in this Jerome Kern biopic.
HIS SONG: 'Ol' Man River' by Jerome Kern and Oscar Hammerstein II.

IT HAPPENED IN BROOKLYN
Metro-Goldwyn-Mayer 1947

Produced by Jack Cummings. Directed by Richard Whorf. Screenplay by Isobel Lennart. Based on an original story by John McGowan. Musical supervision, direction, and incidental score by Johnny Green. Orchestrations by Ted Duncan. Frank Sinatra's vocal orchestrations by Axel Stordahl. Musical numbers staged and directed by Jack Donohue. Piano solos arranged and played by André Previn. Running time: 104 minutes.

WITH Kathryn Grayson, Peter Lawford, Jimmy Durante, and Gloria Grahame.
SINATRA played a GI returning home to his beloved Brooklyn who begins by being in love only with the Brooklyn Bridge and ends up with a girl.
HIS SONGS: 'Brooklyn Bridge', 'I Believe', 'Time After Time', 'The Song's Gotta Come from the Heart', and 'It's the Same Old Dream' by Jule Styne and Sammy Cahn; 'La Ci Darem la Mano' by Mozart; 'Black Eyes' (in Russian).

THE MIRACLE OF THE BELLS
RKO 1948

Produced by Jesse L. Lasky and Walter MacEwen.
Directed by Irving Pichel. Screenplay by Ben Hecht
and Quentin Reynolds. Additional material for Frank
Sinatra's sequences by DeWitt Bodeen. Based on the
novel by Russell Janney. Music by Leigh Harline.
Musical director: Constantin Bakaleinikoff.
Running time: 120 minutes.

WITH Fred MacMurray, Alida Valli, and Lee J. Cobb.
Narrated by Quentin Reynolds.
SINATRA, in this his first dramatic role, played Father
Paul of St Michael's Church.
HIS SONG: 'Ever Homeward' by Kasimierz Lubomirski,
Jule Styne, and Sammy Cahn.

THE KISSING BANDIT
Metro-Goldwyn-Mayer 1948
Technicolor

Produced by Joe Pasternak. Directed by Laslo Benedek.
Original screenplay by Isobel Lennart and John Briard
Harding. Music supervised and conducted by George
Stoll. Musical arrangements by Leo Arnaud. Incidental
score by George Stoll, Albert Sendrey, Scott Bradley,
and André Previn. Additional orchestrations by Albert
Sendrey, Calvin Jackson, Conrad Salinger, Robert Van
Eps, Paul Marquardt, and Earl Brent. Dance director:
Stanley Donen. Running time: 102 minutes.

WITH Kathryn Grayson, J. Carrol Naish, Mildred
Natwick, Mikhail Rasumny, and Billy Gilbert, with
Ricardo Montalban, Ann Miller, and Cyd Charisse in
'Dance of Fury' by Nacio Herb Brown.
SINATRA played Ricardo, who returns to California from
Boston to find that he is expected to take over the
leadership of his father's old bandit gang.
HIS SONGS: 'What's Wrong with Me?', 'If I Steal a Kiss',
and 'Senorita' by Nacio Herb Brown and Edward
Heyman; 'Siesta' by Nacio Herb Brown and Earl Brent.

TAKE ME OUT TO THE BALL GAME
Metro-Goldwyn-Mayer 1949
Technicolor

Produced by Arthur Freed. Directed by Busby
Berkeley. Screenplay by Harry Tugend and George
Wells. Based on a story by Gene Kelly and Stanley
Donen. Music supervised and conducted by Adolph
Deutsch. Incidental score by Roger Edens. Orchestral
arrangements by Adolph Deutsch, Conrad Salinger,
Robert Franklyn, Paul Marquardt, Alexander Courage,
Axel Stordahl, and Leo Arnaud. Vocal arrangements by
Robert Tucker. Dance directors: Gene Kelly and
Stanley Donen. Running time: 93 minutes.

WITH Esther Williams, Gene Kelly, Betty Garrett,
Edward Arnold, Jules Munshin, and Joi Lansing.
SINATRA played Dennis Ryan, one half of a popular
vaudeville song-and-dance team (the other half was
Eddie O'Brien, played by Gene Kelly) who spent every
summer as a star player of the Wolves Baseball Team.
HIS SONGS: 'Take Me Out to the Ball Game' by Albert
von Tilzer and Jack Norworth; 'Yes, Indeedy', 'O'Brien
to Ryan to Goldberg', 'The Right Girl for Me', and 'It's
Fate, Baby, It's Fate' by Roger Edens, Betty Comden,
and Adolph Green; 'Strictly U.S.A.' by Roger Edens.

ON THE TOWN
Metro-Goldwyn-Mayer 1949
Technicolor

Produced by Arthur Freed. Directed by Gene Kelly and Stanley Donen. Screenplay by Adolph Green and Betty Comden, from their musical play based on an idea by Jerome Robbins. Music supervised and conducted by Lennie Hayton. Orchestral arrangements by Conrad Salinger, Robert Franklyn, and Wally Heglin. Vocal arrangements by Saul Chaplin. Incidental score by Roger Edens, Saul Chaplin and Conrad Salinger. Music for 'Miss Turnstiles' Dance and 'A Day in New York' Ballet by Leonard Bernstein. Running time: 98 minutes.

WITH Gene Kelly, Betty Garrett, Ann Miller, Jules Munshin, Vera-Ellen, Florence Bates, and Alice Pearce.
SINATRA played Chip, a sailor on twenty-four hours shore leave in New York, who, with his buddies (Gene Kelly and Jules Munshin), found romance.
HIS SONGS: 'New York, New York' and 'Come Up to My Place' by Leonard Bernstein, Adolph Green, and Betty Comden; 'You're Awful', 'On the Town', and 'Count on Me' by Roger Edens, Adolph Green, and Betty Comden.

MEET DANNY WILSON
Universal-International 1951

Produced by Leonard Goldstein. Directed by Joseph Pevney. Associate producer and original screenplay by Don McGuire. Musical director: Joseph Gershenson. Musical numbers staged by Hal Belfer. Running time: 88 minutes.

WITH Shelley Winters, Alex Nicol, Raymond Burr, and Tony Curtis.
SINATRA played Danny Wilson, a singer who made good in the tough world of nightclubs: a thinly disguised fictional version of his own career.
HIS SONGS: 'You're a Sweetheart' by Jimmy McHugh and Harold Adamson; 'Lonesome Man Blues' by Sy Oliver; 'She's Funny That Way' by Richard Whiting and Neil Moret; 'A Good Man Is Hard to Find' by Eddie Green; 'That Old Black Magic' by Harold Arlen and Johnny Mercer; 'When You're Smiling' by Mark Fisher, Joe Goodwin, and Larry Shay; 'All of Me' by Seymour Simons and Gerald Marks; 'I've Got a Crush on You' by George and Ira Gershwin; 'How Deep Is The Ocean?' by Irving Berlin.

DOUBLE DYNAMITE
RKO 1951

Produced by Irving Cummings Jr. Directed by Irving Cummings. Screenplay by Melville Shavelson. Additional dialogue by Harry Crane. From an original story by Leo Rosten. Music by Leigh Harline. Running time: 80 minutes.

WITH Jane Russell and Groucho Marx.
SINATRA played Johnny Dalton, a bank clerk in love with Jane Russell.
HIS SONGS: 'Kisses and Tears' and 'It's Only Money' by Jule Styne and Sammy Cahn.

FROM HERE TO ETERNITY
Columbia 1953

Produced by Buddy Adler. Directed by Fred
Zinnemann. Screenplay by Daniel Taradash. Based on
the novel by James Jones. Music supervised and
conducted by Morris Stoloff. Background music by
George Dunning. Orchestrations by Arthur Morton.
Song 'Re-enlistment Blues' by James Jones, Fred
Karger, and Robert Wells. Running time: 118 minutes.

WITH Burt Lancaster, Montgomery Clift, Deborah
Kerr, Donna Reed, Philip Ober, Mickey Shaughnessy,
Harry Bellaver, and Ernest Borgnine.
SINATRA played Angelo Maggio, the doomed private
soldier from James Jones's novel.
From Here to Eternity won eight Oscars in the 1953
Academy Awards: best picture, direction, screenplay,
photography, film editing, sound, supporting actesss
(Donna Reed) and supporting actor (Frank Sinatra,
who dropped his top billing to win it).

SUDDENLY
Libra 1954 Released by United Artists

Produced by Robert Bassler. Directed by Lewis Allen.
Original screenplay by Richard Sale. Music by David
Raksin. Running time: 77 minutes.

WITH Sterling Hayden, James Gleason, Nancy Gates,
and Willis Bouchey.
SINATRA played John Baron, a man determined to be
somebody–in this case by becoming a presidential
assassin.

YOUNG AT HEART
Arwin 1955 Released by Warner Bros.
WarnerColor: print by Technicolor

Produced by Henry Blanke. Directed by Gordon
Douglas. Adaptation by Liam O'Brien from the
screenplay *Four Daughters* by Julius J. Epstein and
Lenore Coffee. Music supervised, arranged, and
conducted by Ray Heindorf. Piano solos played by
André Previn. Running time: 117 minutes.

WITH Doris Day, Gig Young, Ethel Barrymore,
Dorothy Malone, Robert Keith, Elisabeth Fraser, and
Alan Hale Jr.
SINATRA played the role of Barney Sloan in this
musical re-make of *Four Daughters* (the original part
was played by John Garfield). Sloan is a moody and
bitter musician who wins Doris Day in the end.
HIS SONGS: 'Young at Heart' by Johnny Richards and
Carolyn Leigh; 'Someone to Watch Over Me' by
George and Ira Gershwin; 'Just One of Those Things'
by Cole Porter; 'One for My Baby' by Harold Arlen
and Johnny Mercer; 'You, My Love' by Mack Gordon
and James Van Heusen.

NOT AS A STRANGER
Stanley Kramer 1955 Released by United Artists

Produced and directed by Stanley Kramer. Screenplay
by Edna and Edward Anhalt. Based on the novel by
Morton Thompson. Music composed and conducted by
George Antheil. Orchestrations by Ernest Gold.
Running time: 135 minutes.

WITH Olivia de Havilland, Robert Mitchum, Gloria
Grahame, Broderick Crawford, Charles Bickford,
Myron McCormick, Lon Chaney, and Lee Marvin.
SINATRA played Dr Alfred Boone, best friend of Robert
Mitchum's Dr Lucas Marsh.

THE TENDER TRAP
Metro-Goldwyn-Mayer 1955
Eastman Color: CinemaScope

Produced by Lawrence Weingarten. Directed by
Charles Walters. Screenplay by Julius J. Epstein.
Based on the play by Max Shulman and Robert Paul
Smith. Music composed and conducted by Jeff
Alexander. Orchestrations by Will Beittel.
Running time: 111 minutes.

WITH Debbie Reynolds, David Wayne, Celeste Holm,
Jarma Lewis, Lola Albright, and Carolyn Jones.
SINATRA played Charlie Y. Reader, a swinging New
York theatrical agent.
HIS SONG: '(Love Is) The Tender Trap' by James Van
Heusen and Sammy Cahn.

GUYS AND DOLLS
Samuel Goldwyn 1955 Released by Metro-Goldwyn-Mayer
Eastman Color: CinemaScope

Produced by Samuel Goldwyn. Directed by Joseph L.
Mankiewicz. Screenplay by Joseph L. Mankiewicz.
From the musical play: book by Jo Swerling and Abe
Burrows; music and lyrics by Frank Loesser. Based on
the story 'The Idyll of Miss Sarah Brown' by Damon
Runyon. Music supervised and conducted by Jay
Blackton. Orchestral arrangements by Skip Martin,
Nelson Riddle (for Sinatra), Alexander Courage, and
Albert Sendrey. Choreography by Michael Kidd.
Running time: 150 minutes.

WITH Marlon Brando, Jean Simmons, Vivian Blaine,
Robert Keith, Stubby Kaye, B.S. Pully, Johnny Silver,
Sheldon Leonard, Dan Dayton, George E. Stone, and
Regis Toomey.
SINATRA played Nathan Detroit, who ran 'the oldest
established, permanent floating crap game in New
York'.
HIS SONGS: 'The Oldest Established (Permanent
Floating Crap Game in New York)', 'Guys and Dolls',
'Adelaide', and 'Sue Me', all by Frank Loesser.

THE MAN WITH THE GOLDEN ARM
Carlyle 1955 Released by United Artists

Produced and directed by Otto Preminger. Screenplay by Walter Newman and Lewis Meltzer. Based on the novel by Nelson Algren. Music composed and conducted by Elmer Bernstein. Orchestrations by Frederick Steiner. Running time: 119 minutes.

WITH Eleanor Parker, Kim Novak, Arnold Stang, Darren McGavin, and Robert Strauss.
SINATRA played drug-addicted jazz drummer Frankie Machine.
Sinatra received an Academy nomination for Best Actor: the award went to Ernest Borgnine for *Marty*.

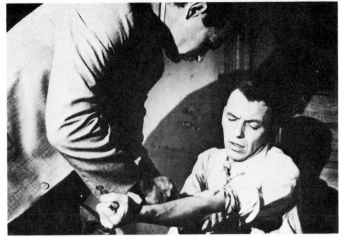

MEET ME IN LAS VEGAS
Metro-Goldwyn-Mayer 1956
Eastman Color: CinemaScope

Produced by Joe Pasternak. Directed by Roy Rowland. Original screenplay by Isobel Lennart. Running time: 112 minutes.

WITH Dan Dailey, Cyd Charisse, Jerry Colonna, Paul Henreid, Lena Horne, Frankie Laine, Agnes Moorhead, and unbilled guests Debbie Reynolds, Tony Martin, Peter Lorre, Vic Damone, and Elaine Stewart.
SINATRA played himself in an unbilled guest appearance.

JOHNNY CONCHO
Kent 1956 Released by United Artists

Produced by Frank Sinatra. Associate producer: Henry Sanicola. Directed by Don McGuire, associate producer and writer of *Meet Danny Wilson*. Screenplay by David P. Harmon and Don McGuire. Based on the story 'The Man Who Owned the Town' by David P. Harmon. Music composed and conducted by Nelson Riddle. Orchestrations by Arthur Morton. Running time: 84 minutes.

WITH Keenan Wynn, William Conrad, Phyllis Kirk, and Wallace Ford.
SINATRA played the title role, a gunman trying to match up to the killer reputation of his dead brother in this the first film he produced.

HIGH SOCIETY
Metro-Goldwyn-Mayer 1956
Technicolor: VistaVision

Produced by Sol C. Siegel. Directed by Charles Walters. Screenplay by John Patrick. Based on the play *The Philadelphia Story* by Philip Barry. Music supervised and adapted by Johnny Green and Saul Chaplin. Orchestra conducted by Johnny Green. Orchestral arrangements by Conrad Salinger and Nelson Riddle. Additional orchestrations by Robert Franklyn and Albert Sendrey. Musical numbers staged by Charles Walters. Running time: 107 minutes.

WITH Bing Crosby, Grace Kelly, Celeste Holm, John Lund, Louis Calhern, Sidney Blackmer, Louis Armstrong, Margalo Gillmore, and Lydia Reed.
SINATRA played journalist Mike Connor in a musical version of *The Philadelphia Story*.
HIS SONGS: 'Who Wants to Be a Millionaire?', 'You're Sensational', 'Well, Did You Evah?', and 'Mind If I Make Love to You?', all by Cole Porter.

AROUND THE WORLD IN 80 DAYS
Michael Todd 1956 Released by United Artists
Eastman Color: Print by Technicolor: Todd-AO

Produced by Michael Todd. Associate producer:
William Cameron Menzies. Directed by Michael
Anderson. Screenplay by James Poe, John Farrow,
and S. J. Perelman. Based on the novel by Jules
Verne. Music by Victor Young. Running time:
178 minutes.

WITH David Niven, Cantinflas, Shirley MacLaine, and
Robert Newton.
SINATRA made a cameo appearance as a piano player
in a Barbary Coast saloon.

THE PRIDE AND THE PASSION
Stanley Kramer 1957 Released by United Artists
Technicolor: VistaVision

Produced and directed by Stanley Kramer. Screenplay
by Edna and Edward Anhalt. Based on the novel *The
Gun* by C. S. Forester. Music by George Antheil;
orchestrated and conducted by Ernest Gold.
Running time: 132 minutes.

WITH Cary Grant, Sophia Loren, Theodore Bikel, John
Wengraf, and Jay Novello.
SINATRA played Miguel, a peasant and Spanish
guerrilla fighter.

THE JOKER IS WILD
A.M.B.L. 1957 Released by Paramount
VistaVision

Produced by Samuel J. Briskin. Directed by Charles
Vidor. Screenplay by Oscar Saul. Based on the book
by Art Cohn. Music composed and conducted by
Walter Scharf. Orchestrations by Leo Shuken and
Jack Hayes. Orchestral arrangements of songs by
Nelson Riddle. Specialty songs and parodies by Harry
Harris. Dances staged by Josephine Earl.
Running time: 126 minutes.

WITH Mitzi Gaynor, Jeanne Crain, Eddie Albert,
Beverly Garland, Jackie Coogan, and Sophie Tucker.
SINATRA played nightclub entertainer Joe E. Lewis in
the biopic of the performer.
HIS SONGS: 'I Cried for You' by Arthur Freed, Gus
Arnheim, and Abe Lyman; 'If I Could Be with You' by
Jimmy Johnson and Henry Creamer; 'Chicago' by
Fred Fisher; 'All the Way' by James Van Heusen and
Sammy Cahn (Academy Award for Best Song of 1957).

PAL JOEY
Essex-George Sidney 1957 Released by Columbia
Technicolor

Produced by Fred Kohlmar. Directed by George
Sidney. Screenplay by Dorothy Kingsley. Based on the
musical play by John O'Hara (book), Richard Rodgers
(music), and Lorenz Hart (lyrics). Music supervised
and conducted by Morris Stoloff. Musical
arrangements by Nelson Riddle. Music adaptation by
George Duning and Nelson Riddle. Orchestrations by
Arthur Morton. Choreography by Hermes Pan.
Running time: 111 minutes.

WITH Rita Hayworth, Kim Novak, Barbara Nichols,
Hank Henry, and Hermes Pan.
SINATRA played the title role, Joey Evans, an out-and-
out heel of a nightclub singer.
HIS SONGS: 'I Didn't Know What Time It Was',
'There's a Small Hotel', 'I Could Write a Book', 'The
Lady Is a Tramp', 'Bewitched, Bothered and
Bewildered', and 'What Do I Care for a Dame?', all by
Richard Rodgers and Lorenz Hart.

KINGS GO FORTH
Frank Ross-Eton 1958 Released by United Artists

Produced by Frank Ross. Directed by Delmer Daves.
Screenplay by Merle Miller. Based on the novel by
Joe David Brown. Music composed and conducted by
Elmer Bernstein. Orchestrations by Leo Shuken and
Jack Hayes. Running time: 109 minutes.

WITH Tony Curtis, Natalie Wood, and Leora Dana.
SINATRA played Lt. Sam Loggins, an American soldier
from the South who falls in love with a girl who is the
product of a mixed marriage.

SOME CAME RUNNING
Metro-Goldwyn-Mayer 1958
MetroColor: CinemaScope

Produced by Sol C. Siegel. Directed by Vincente
Minnelli. Screenplay by John Patrick and Arthur
Sheekman. Based on the novel by James Jones, the
man who wrote *From Here to Eternity*. Music
composed and conducted by Elmer Bernstein.
Orchestrations by Leo Shuken and Jack Hayes. Song
'To Love and Be Loved' by James Van Heusen and
Sammy Cahn. Running time: 127 minutes.

WITH Dean Martin, Shirley MacLaine, Martha Hyer,
Arthur Kennedy, Nancy Gates, Leora Dana, and
Betty Lou Keim.
SINATRA played Dave Hirsh, discharged from the army
and returning as a would-be writer to his home town
in Indiana.

A HOLE IN THE HEAD

Sincap 1959 Released by United Artists
Color by DeLuxe: CinemaScope

Produced and directed by Frank Capra. Screenplay by
Arnold Schulman, based on his play. Music by Nelson
Riddle. Running time: 120 minutes.

WITH Edward G. Robinson, Eleanor Parker, Carolyn
Jones, Thelma Ritter, Keenan Wynn, Eddie Hodges,
and Joi Lansing.
SINATRA played a widower, father, and ne'er-do-well
hotel proprietor in Miami.
HIS SONGS: 'All My Tomorrows' and 'High Hopes',
both by James Van Heusen and Sammy Cahn. 'High
Hopes' won the Academy Award for Best Song of 1959.

NEVER SO FEW

Canterbury 1959 Released by Metro-Goldwyn-Mayer
Metrocolor: CinemaScope

Produced by Edmund Grainger. Directed by John
Sturges. Screenplay by Millard Kaufman. Based on
the novel by Tom T. Chamales. Music by Hugo
Friedhofer; orchestrated by Robert Franklyn.
Running time: 124 minutes.

WITH Gina Lollobrigida, Peter Lawford, Steve
McQueen, Richard Johnson, Paul Henreid, Brian
Donlevy, Dean Jones, Charles Bronson, and
Philip Ahn.
SINATRA played Captain Tom C. Reynolds, leader of a
band of guerrilla fighters opposing the Japanese in
Burma in World War Two.

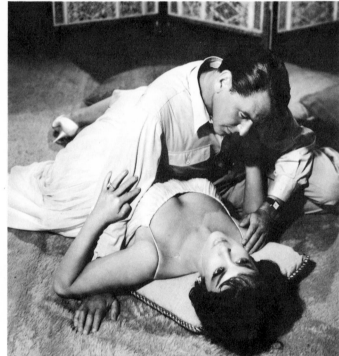

CAN-CAN

Suffolk-Cummings 1960 Released by Twentieth Century-Fox
Technicolor: Todd-AO

Produced by Jack Cummings. Associate producer:
Saul Chaplin. Directed by Walter Lang. Screenplay by
Dorothy Kingsley and Charles Lederer. Based on the
musical play by Abe Burrows. Songs by Cole Porter.
Music arranged and conducted by Nelson Riddle.
Vocal supervision by Bobby Tucker. Dances staged by
Hermes Pan. Running time: 130 minutes.

WITH Shirley MacLaine, Maurice Chevalier, Louis
Jourdan, Juliet Prowse, and Marcel Dalio.
SINATRA played Parisian lawyer François Durnais,
stern opponent of the law forbidding the Can-Can.
HIS SONGS: 'I Love Paris', 'C'est Magnifique', 'Let's Do
It', and 'It's All Right with Me', all by Cole Porter.

OCEAN'S ELEVEN
Dorchester 1960 Released by Warner Bros.
Technicolor: Panavision

Produced and directed by Lewis Milestone. Associate producers: Henry Sanicola and Milton Ebbins. Screenplay by Harry Brown and Charles Lederer. Based on an original story by George Clayton Johnson and Jack Golden Russell. Music composed and conducted by Nelson Riddle. Orchestrations by Arthur Morton. Songs 'Ain't That a Kick in the Head' and 'Eee-o Eleven' by James Van Heusen and Sammy Cahn. Running time: 127 minutes.

WITH Dean Martin, Sammy Davis Jr, Peter Lawford, Angie Dickinson, Richard Conte, Cesar Romero, Patrice Wymore, Joey Bishop, Akim Tamiroff, Henry Silva, Red Skelton, George Raft, and Shirley MacLaine.
SINATRA played Danny Ocean, the leader of a gang setting out to rob five Las Vegas casinos.

SERGEANTS THREE
Essex-Claude 1962 Released by United Artists
Technicolor: Panavision

Produced by Frank Sinatra. Executive producer: Howard W. Koch. Directed by John Sturges. Original screenplay by W. R. Burnett. Music by Billy May. Song 'And the Night Wind Sang' by Johnny Rotella and Franz Steininger. Running time: 112 minutes.

WITH Dean Martin, Sammy Davis Jr, Peter Lawford, Joey Bishop, Henry Silva, Ruta Lee, Buddy Lester, Phillip Crosby, Dennis Crosby, Lindsay Crosby, and Hank Henry.
SINATRA played 1st Sergeant Mike Merry in a Western re-make of Gunga Din.

PEPE
G.S.-Posa Films International 1960 Released by Columbia
Technicolor

Produced and directed by George Sidney. Screenplay by Dorothy Kingsley and Claude Binyon. From a story by Leonard Spigelgass and Sonya Levien. Based on the play *Broadway Magic* by Ladislas Bush-Fekete. Running time: 195 minutes.

WITH Cantinflas, Dan Dailey, Shirley Jones, and twenty-six other guest stars and personalities.
SINATRA made a guest appearance as himself.

THE DEVIL AT 4 O'CLOCK
Columbia 1961
Eastman Color

Produced by Fred Kohlmar. Directed by Mervyn LeRoy. Screenplay by Liam O'Brien. Based on the novel by Max Catto. Music by George Duning; orchestrated by Arthur Morton. Running time: 126 minutes.

WITH Spencer Tracy, Kerwin Mathews, Jean Pierre Aumont, Gregoire Aslan, Alexander Scourby, and Barbara Luna.
SINATRA played a convict, Harry, who helped Spencer Tracy (Father Matthew Doonan) to save the lives of children threatened by an erupting volcano.

THE ROAD TO HONG KONG
Melnor Films 1962 Released by United Artists

Produced by Melvin Frank. Directed by Norman Panama. Original screenplay by Norman Panama and Melvin Frank. Music composed and conducted by Robert Farnon. Running time: 91 minutes.

WITH Bing Crosby, Bob Hope, Joan Collins, Dorothy Lamour, and Robert Morley.
SINATRA played a comic spaceman (with Dean Martin) in an unbilled guest appearance.

THE MANCHURIAN CANDIDATE
M.C. Production 1962 Released by United Artists

Produced by George Axelrod and John Frankenheimer. Directed by John Frankenheimer. Executive producer: Howard W. Koch. Screenplay by George Axelrod. Based on the novel by Richard Condon. Music composed and conducted by David Amram. Running time: 126 minutes.

WITH Laurence Harvey, Janet Leigh, Angela Lansbury, Henry Silva, James Gregory, Leslie Parrish, John McGiver, Knigh Dhiegh, James Edwards, Douglas Henderson, and Albert Paulsen.
SINATRA played Army Intelligence Officer Bennett Marco, trying to prevent 'programmed' ex-soldier Laurence Harvey from assassinating the presidential nominee at a rally.

THE LIST OF ADRIAN MESSENGER
Joel 1963 Released by Universal

Produced by Edward Lewis. Directed by John Huston. Screenplay by Anthony Veiller. Based on the novel by Philip MacDonald. Music by Jerry Goldsmith. Running time: 98 minutes.

WITH George C. Scott, Dana Wynter, Clive Brook, Gladys Cooper, Herbert Marshall, and, as guest stars in disguise, Tony Curtis, Kirk Douglas, Burt Lancaster, and Robert Mitchum.
SINATRA guest starred disguised as a gipsy stable man.

COME BLOW YOUR HORN
Essex-Tandem 1963 Released by Paramount
Technicolor: Panavision

Produced by Norman Lear and Bud Yorkin. Executive producer: Howard W. Koch. Directed by Bud Yorkin. Screenplay by Norman Lear. Based on the play by Neil Simon. Music composed and conducted by Nelson Riddle. Orchestrations by Gil Grau. Running time: 112 minutes.

WITH Lee J. Cobb, Molly Picon, Barbara Rush, Jill St John, Tony Bill, Dan Blocker, Phyllis McGuire and Dean Martin.
SINATRA played swinging bachelor Alan Baker.
HIS SONG: 'Come Blow Your Horn' by James Van Heusen and Sammy Cahn.

FOUR FOR TEXAS
Sam 1964 Released by Warner Bros.
Technicolor

Produced and directed by Robert Aldrich. Executive producer: Howard W. Koch. Original screenplay by Teddi Sherman and Robert Aldrich. Music composed and conducted by Nelson Riddle. Orchestrations by Gil Grau. Title song by James Van Heusen and Sammy Cahn. Running time: 124 minutes.

WITH Dean Martin, Anita Ekberg, Ursula Andress, Charles Bronson, Victor Buono, Edric Connor, Nick Dennis, Richard Jaeckel, Mike Mazurki, Wesley Addy, and special guest stars, the Three Stooges.
SINATRA played Zack Thomas in this comedy Western.

ROBIN AND THE SEVEN HOODS
P-C Productions 1964 Released by Warner Bros.
Technicolor: Panavision

Produced by Frank Sinatra. Executive producer: Howard W. Koch. Directed by Gordon Douglas. Original screenplay by David R. Schwartz. Music composed and conducted by Nelson Riddle. Orchestrations by Gil Grau. Associate producer and director of photography: William H. Daniels. Choreographer for dances: Jack Baker. Running time: 123 minutes.

WITH Dean Martin, Sammy Davis Jr, Peter Falk, Barbara Rush, Victor Buono, Hank Henry, Allen Jenkins, Jack La Rue, Phillip Crosby, Edward G. Robinson, and Bing Crosby.
SINATRA played Robbo in a spoof of the Robin Hood legend set in 1928 Chicago during the gangster prohibition wars.
HIS SONGS: 'My Kind of Town', 'Style', 'Mr Booze', and 'Don't Be a Do-Badder', all by James Van Heusen and Sammy Cahn.

NONE BUT THE BRAVE
Artanis 1965 Released by Warner Bros.
Technicolor: Panavision

Produced and directed by Frank Sinatra. Executive producer: Howard W. Koch. Associate producer: William H. Daniels. Producer for Tokyo Eiga Company and original story by Kikumaru Okuda. Screenplay by John Twist and Katsuya Susaki. Music composed by Johnny Williams. Music supervised and conducted by Morris Stoloff. Japanese music adviser: K. Hirose. Running time: 105 minutes.

WITH Clint Walker, Tommy Sands, Brad Dexter, Tony Bill, Tatsuya Mihashi, Takeshi Kato, and Phillip Crosby.
SINATRA played Chief Pharmacist Mate Maloney in this war drama set on a small Pacific island.

VON RYAN'S EXPRESS
P-R Production 1965 Released by Twentieth Century-Fox
Color by DeLuxe: CinemaScope

Produced by Saul David. Directed by Mark Robson.
Screenplay by Wendell Mayes and Joseph Landon.
Based on the novel by David Westheimer. Music by
Jerry Goldsmith. Orchestrations by Arthur Morton.
Running time: 117 minutes.

WITH Trevor Howard, Raffaella Carra, Brad Dexter,
Sergio Fantoni, John Leyton, Edward Mulhare,
Wolfgang Preiss, James Brolin, John Van Dreelen,
and Adolfo Celi.
SINATRA played US Colonel Joseph L. Ryan, the leader
of a daring prisoner-of-war escape in World War Two.

MARRIAGE ON THE ROCKS
A-C Productions 1965 Released by Warner Bros.
Technicolor: Panavision

Producer and director of photography: William H.
Daniels. Directed by Jack Donohue. Original
screenplay by Cy Howard. Music composed and
conducted by Nelson Riddle. Song 'Sinner Man' by
Trini Lopez, Bobby Weinstein, Bobby Hart, Billy
Barberis, and Teddy Randazzo. Running time:
109 minutes.

WITH Deborah Kerr, Dean Martin, Cesar Romero,
Hermione Baddeley, Tony Bill, John McGiver, Nancy
Sinatra, Joi Lansing, and guest star Trini Lopez.
SINATRA played Dan Edwards, president of an
advertising agency who goes to Mexico to celebrate
his nineteenth wedding anniversary to Deborah Kerr
and ends up being divorced by mistake.

THE OSCAR
Greene-Rouse 1966 Released by Embassy Pictures
Pathé Color

Produced by Clarence Greene. Directed by Russell
Rouse. Executive producer: Joseph E. Levine.
Screenplay by Harlan Ellison, Russell Rouse, and
Clarence Greene. Based on the novel by Richard Sale.
Music by Percy Faith. Orchestrations by Leo Shuken
and Jack Hayes. Songs 'Thanks for the Memory' by
Ralph Rainger and Leo Robin; 'All the Way' by James
Van Heusen and Sammy Cahn. Running time:
119 minutes.

WITH Stephen Boyd, Elke Sommer, Milton Berle,
Eleanor Parker, Joseph Cotten, Jill St John, Tony
Bennett, and Edie Adams.
SINATRA appeared as himself in a scene set at the
Oscar presentations.

CAST A GIANT SHADOW
Mirisch-Llenroc-Batjac 1966 Released by United Artists
Color by DeLuxe: Panavision

Produced and directed by Melville Shavelson. Co-
producer: Michael Wayne. Screenplay by Melvill
Shavelson. Based on the book by Ted Berkman. Music
composed and conducted by Elmer Bernstein.
Orchestrations by Leo Shuken and Jack Hayes.
Running time: 139 minutes.

WITH Kirk Douglas, Senta Berger, Angie Dickinson,
James Donald, Stathis Giallelis, Luther Adler, Gary
Merrill, and Haym Topol.
SINATRA played Vince, a New Jersey pilot of fortune
in a guest appearance alongside Yul Brynner and
John Wayne.

ASSAULT ON A QUEEN
Sinatra Enterprises-Seven Arts 1966 Released by Paramount
Technicolor: Panavision

Produced by William Goetz. Directed by Jack
Donohue. Screenplay by Rod Serling. Based on the
novel by Jack Finney. Music by Duke Ellington.
Orchestral arrangements by Van Cleave and Frank
Comstock. Associate producer and director of
photography: William H. Daniels. Running time:
106 minutes.

WITH Virna Lisi, Tony Franciosa, Richard Conte, Alf
Kjellin, Errol John, Murray Matheson, and
Reginald Denny.
SINATRA played Mark Brittain, a member of a group
planning to hijack the *Queen Mary* from a submarine.

THE NAKED RUNNER
Sinatra Enterprises 1967 Released by Warner Bros.
Technicolor: Techniscope

Produced by Brad Dexter. Directed by Sidney J. Furie.
Screenplay by Stanley Mann. Based on the novel by
Francis Clifford. Music by Harry Sukman.
Orchestrations by Herbert Spencer. Running time:
103 minutes.

WITH Peter Vaughan, Derren Nesbitt, Nadia Gray,
Toby Robins, Inger Stratton, Cyril Luckham, and
Edward Fox.
SINATRA played Sam Laker, a widowed American
businessman living in London and involved in a
complicated espionage plot.

TONY ROME
Arcola-Millfield 1967 Released by Twentieth Century-Fox
Color by DeLuxe: Panavision

Produced by Aaron Rosenberg. Directed by Gordon
Douglas. Screenplay by Richard L. Breen. Based on
the novel *Miami Mayhem* by Martin H. Albert. Music
by Billy May. Title song by Lee Hazlewood, sung by
Nancy Sinatra; 'Something Here Inside of Me' by
Billy May and Randy Newman. Running time:
110 minutes.

WITH Jill St John, Richard Conte, Gena Rowlands,
Simon Oakland, Jeffrey Lynn, Lloyd Bochner, Robert
J. Wilke, Michael Romanoff, Diana Pines, and
Sue Lyon.
SINATRA played the title role, a Miami private eye
involved in a complex murder case.

THE DETECTIVE
Arcola-Millfield 1968 Released by Twentieth Century-Fox
Color by DeLuxe: Panavision

Produced by Aaron Rosenberg. Directed by Gordon
Douglas. Screenplay by Abby Mann. Based on the
novel by Roderick Thorp. Music by Jerry Goldsmith.
Orchestration by Warren Barker. Running time:
114 minutes.

WITH Lee Remick, Ralph Meeker, Jack Klugman,
Horace McMahon, Lloyd Bochner, William Windom,
Tony Musante, Al Freeman Jr, Robert Duvall, Pat
Henry, Sugar Ray Robinson, and Jacqueline Bisset.
SINATRA played New York homicide detective Joe
Leland, leading the police for the brutal slaying of a
homosexual.

LADY IN CEMENT
Arcola-Millfield 1968 Released by Twentieth Century-Fox
Color by DeLuxe: Panavision

Produced by Aaron Rosenberg. Directed by Gordon
Douglas. Screenplay by Marvin H. Albert and Jack
Guss. Based on the novel by Martin H. Albert. Music
composed and conducted by Hugo Montenegro.
Orchestration by Billy May. Underwater sequence
staged by Riccou Browning. Running time:
93 minutes.

WITH Raquel Welch, Dan Blocker, Richard Conte,
Martin Gabel, Lainie Kazan, and Pat Henry.
SINATRA reprised his role as Miami private eye
Tony Rome.

DIRTY DINGUS MAGEE
Metro-Goldwyn-Mayer 1970
MetroColor: Panavision

Produced and directed by Burt Kennedy. Screenplay
by Tom & Frank Waldman and Joseph Heller. Based
on the novel *The Ballad of Dingus Magee* by David
Markson. Music by Jeff Alexander; additional music
by Billy Strange. Title song by Mack David, sung by
the Mike Curb Congregation. Running time:
91 minutes.

WITH George Kennedy, Anne Jackson, Lois Nettleton,
Jack Elam, John Dehner, and Henry Jones.
SINATRA played the title role as a thieving cowboy in
this comedy Western.

CONTRACT ON CHERRY STREET
Artanis in association with Columbia TV 1977

Produced by Hugh Benson. Executive producer: Renee
Valente. Directed by William A. Graham. Written by
Edward Anhalt. Based on the best-seller by Phillip
Rosenberg. Music by Jerry Goldsmith. Running time:
148 minutes.

WITH Martin Balsam, Jay Black, Verna Bloom, Joe De
Santis, Martin Gabel, Harry Guardino, James Luisi,
Michael Nouri, Marco St John, Henry Silva, and
Richard Ward.
SINATRA played Detective Frank Hovannes, a veteran
New York cop who goes underground to break up the
crime syndicates.

Selected Discography

The following represents only a small part of an incredible recording output. I have deliberately chosen only those LPs which are considered to be the key albums of Sinatra's career.

Columbia

FRANKIE
Columbia CL 606
With various arrangers and conductors

Hello, Young Lovers
I Only Have Eyes For You
Falling In Love With Love
You'll Never Know
It All Depends On You
S'posin'
All Of Me
Time After Time
How Cute You Can Be
Almost Like Being In Love
Nancy
Oh What It Seemed To Be

THE VOICE
Columbia CL 743
With various arrangers and conductors

I Don't Know Why
Try A Little Tenderness
A Ghost Of A Chance
Paradise
These Foolish Things
Laura
She's Funny That Way
Fools Rush In
Over The Rainbow
That Old Black Magic
Spring Is Here
Lover

ADVENTURES OF THE HEART
Columbia CL 953
With various arrangers and conductors

I Guess I'll Have To Dream The Rest
If Only She'd Look My Way
Love Me
Nevertheless
We Kiss In A Shadow
I Am Loved
Take My Love
I Could Write A Book
Mad About You
Sorry
Stromboli
It's Only A Paper Moon

CHRISTMAS DREAMING
Columbia CL 1032
Arranged and conducted by Axel Stordahl

White Christmas
Jingle Bells
O Little Town Of Bethlehem
Have Yourself A Merry Little Christmas
Christmas Dreaming
Silent Night
It Came Upon The Midnight Clear
Adeste Fideles
Santa Claus Is Comin' To Town
Let It Snow, Let It Snow, Let It Snow

THE FRANK SINATRA STORY IN MUSIC
Columbia CL 1130
With various arrangers and conductors

Ciribiribin
All Or Nothing At All
You'll Never Know
If You Are But A Dream
Nancy
You Go To My Head
Stormy Weather
The House I Live In
If I Loved You
Soliloquy
How Deep Is The Ocean?
Ol' Man River

THE FRANK SINATRA STORY IN MUSIC
Columbia CL 1131
With various arrangers and conductors

You'll Never Walk Alone
I Concentrate On You
Castle Rock
Why Was I Born?
I've Got A Crush On You
Begin The Beguine
The Birth Of The Blues
April In Paris
I'm Glad There Is You
Laura
One For My Baby
Put Your Dreams Away

NOTE: These two FRANK SINATRA STORY IN MUSIC discs were a set, C2L6.

PUT YOUR DREAMS AWAY
Columbia CL 1136
Arranged and conducted by Axel Stordahl

I Dream Of You
Dream
I Have But One Heart
The Girl That I Marry
The Things We Did Last Summer
Lost In The Stars
If I Forget You
Mam'selle
The Song Is You
It Never Entered My Mind
Ain'tcha Ever Comin' Back?
Put Your Dreams Away

LOVE IS A KICK
Columbia CL 1241
With various arrangers and conductors

You Do Something To Me
Bim Bam Baby
My Blue Heaven
When You're Smiling
Saturday Night
Bye Bye Baby
The Continental
Deep Night
Should I?
American Beauty Rose
Five Minutes More
Farewell, Farewell To Love

THE BROADWAY KICK
Columbia CL 1297
With various arrangers and conductors

There's No Business Like Show Business
They Say It's Wonderful
Some Enchanted Evening
You're My Girl
Lost In The Stars
Why Can't You Behave?
I Whistle A Happy Tune
The Girl That I Marry
Can't You Just See Yourself?
There But For You Go I
Bali Ha'i
Bess, Oh Where's My Bess?

COME BACK TO SORRENTO
Columbia CL 1359
Arranged and conducted by Axel Stordahl

When The Sun Goes Down
None But The Lonely Heart
Luna Rossa
My Melancholy Baby
Embraceable You
Day By Day
Come Back To Sorrento
I Hear A Rhapsody
Someone To Watch Over Me
September Song
Among My Souvenirs
Always

REFLECTIONS
Columbia CL 1448
With various arrangers and conductors

Stella By Starlight
But Beautiful
Body And Soul
Where Or When?
When Your Lover Has Gone
Strange Music
Goodnight, Irene
Dear Little Boy Of Mine
Mighty Lak' A Rose
The Cradle Song
Nature Boy
All The Things You Are

GREATEST HITS, THE EARLY YEARS, VOLUME I
Columbia CL 2474
With various arrangers and conductors

I've Got A Crush On You
If You Are But A Dream
Nancy
The Girl That I Marry
The House I Live In
Dream
Saturday Night
Five Minutes More
The Coffee Song
Sunday, Monday Or Always
Put Your Dreams Away

GREATEST HITS, THE EARLY YEARS, VOLUME II
Columbia CL 2572
With various arrangers and conductors

Mean To Me
I Have But One Heart
The Moon Was Yellow
Full Moon And Empty Arms
Time After Time
I'm A Fool To Want You
Day By Day
I Couldn't Sleep A Wink Last Night
Ol' Man River
People Will Say We're In Love
September Song

THE ESSENTIAL FRANK SINATRA, VOLUME I
Columbia CL 2739
With various arrangers and conductors

From The Bottom Of My Heart
Melancholy Mood
My Buddy
Here Comes The Night
Close To You
There's No You
The Charm Of You
When Your Lover Has Gone
I Should Care
A Friend Of Yours
My Shawl
Nancy
You Are Too Beautiful
Why Should I?
One Love
Something Old, Something New

THE ESSENTIAL FRANK SINATRA, VOLUME II
Columbia CL 2740
With various arrangers and conductors

Blue Skies
Guess I'll Hang My Tears Out To Dry
Why Shouldn't It Happen To Us?
It's The Same Old Dream
You Can Take My Word For It, Baby
My Romance (with Dinah Shore)
One For My Baby
It All Came True
Poinciana
Body And Soul
I Went Down To Virginia
If I Only Had A Match
Everybody Loves Somebody
Comme Ci, Comme Ca
If You Stub Your Toe On The Moon

THE ESSENTIAL FRANK SINATRA, VOLUME III
Columbia CL 2741
With various arrangers and conductors

The Right Girl For Me
The Hucklebuck
If I Ever Love Again

Why Remind Me?
Sunshine Cake (with Paula Kelly)
Sure Thing
It's Only A Paper Moon
My Blue Heaven
Nevertheless
You're The One
Love Me
I'm A Fool To Want You
The Birth Of The Blues
Walkin' In The Sunshine
Azure-te
Why Try To Change Me Now?

NOTE: The three ESSENTIAL FRANK SINATRA discs were a boxed set No. S3L42; in stereo form, the numbers are CS 9539, CS 9540, CS 9541, the set being numbered S3S42

IN HOLLYWOOD 1943–1949
Columbia CL 2913
With various arrangers and conductors

I Couldn't Sleep A Wink Last Night
The Music Stopped
A Lovely Way To Spend An Evening
I Begged Her
What Makes The Sunset?
I Fall In Love Too Easily
The Charm Of You
The House I Live In
Time After Time
It's The Same Old Dream
The Brooklyn Bridge
I Believe
Ever Homeward
Senorita
If I Steal A Kiss
The Right Girl For Me

THAT OLD FEELING
Columbia CL 902
With various arrangers and conductors

That Old Feeling
Blue Skies
Autumn In New York
Don't Cry, Joe
The Nearness Of You
That Lucky Old Sun
Full Moon And Empty Arms
Once In Love With Amy
A Fellow Needs A Girl
Poinciana
For Every Man There's A Woman
Mean To Me

Capitol

SONGS FOR YOUNG LOVERS
Capitol W 1432
Arranged and conducted by Nelson Riddle

The Girl Next Door
They Can't Take That Away From Me
Violets For Your Furs
Someone To Watch Over Me
My One And Only Love
Little Girl Blue
Like Someone In Love
A Foggy Day
It Worries Me
I Can Read Between The Lines
I Get A Kick Out Of You
My Funny Valentine

THIS IS SINATRA
Capitol T 768
Arranged and conducted by Nelson Riddle

I've Got The World On A String

Three Coins In The Fountain
Love And Marriage
From Here To Eternity
South Of The Border
Rain
The Gal That Got Away
Young At Heart
Learnin' The Blues
My One And Only Love
The Tender Trap
Don't Worry 'Bout Me

NOTE: 'South of The Border' was not arranged and conducted by Billy May as stated on the sleeve.

IN THE WEE SMALL HOURS
Capitol W 581
Arranged and conducted by Nelson Riddle

In The Wee Small Hours Of The Morning
Mood Indigo
Glad To Be Unhappy
I Get Along Without You Very Well
Deep In A Dream
I See Your Face Before Me
Can't We Be Friends?
When Your Love Has Gone
What Is This Thing Called Love?
Last Night When We Were Young
I'll Be Around
Ill Wind
It Never Entered My Mind
Dancing On The Ceiling
I'll Never Be The Same
This Love Of Mine

SONGS FOR SWINGIN' LOVERS
Capitol W 653
Arranged and conducted by Nelson Riddle

You Make Me Feel So Young
It Happened In Monterey
You're Getting To Be A Habit With Me
You Brought A New Kind of Love To Me
Too Marvellous For Words
Old Devil Moon
Pennies From Heaven
Love Is Here To Stay
I've Got You Under My Skin
I Thought About You
We'll Be Together Again
Makin' Whoopee
Swingin' Down The Lane
Anything Goes
How About You?

CLOSE TO YOU
Capitol W 789
Arranged and conducted by Nelson Riddle

Close To You
P.S. I Love You
Love Locked Out
Everything Happens To Me
It's Easy To Remember
Don't Like Goodbyes
With Every Breath I Take
Blame It On My Youth
It Could Happen To You
I've Had My Moments
I Couldn't Sleep A Wink Last Night
The End Of A Love Affair

A SWINGIN' AFFAIR
Capitol W 803
Arranged and conducted by Nelson Riddle

Night And Day

I Wish I Were In Love Again
I Got Plenty O' Nuttin'
I Guess I'll Have To Change My Plan
Nice Work If You Can Get It
Stars Fell on Alabama
No One Ever Tells You
I Won't Dance
The Lonesome Road
At Long Last Love
You'd Be So Nice To Come Home To
I Got It Bad And That Ain't Good
From This Moment On
If I Had You
Oh Look At Me Now

WHERE ARE YOU?
Capitol SW 855
Arranged and conducted by Gordon Jenkins

Where Are You?
The Night We Called It A Day
I Cover The Waterfront
Maybe You'll Be There
Laura
Lonely Town
Autumn Leaves
I'm A Fool To Want You
I Think of You
Where Is The One?
There's No You
Baby, Won't You Please Come Home?

NOTE: The original stereo issue did not include 'I Cover the Waterfront'.

THIS IS SINATRA, VOLUME II
Capitol W 982
Arranged and conducted by Nelson Riddle

Hey, Jealous Lover
Everybody Loves Somebody
Something Wonderful Happens In Summer
Half As Lovely
You're Cheatin' Yourself
You'll Always Be The One I Love
You Forget All The Words
How Little We Know
Time After Time
Crazy Love
Wait For Me
If You Are But A Dream
So Long My Love
It's The Same Old Dream
I Believe
Put Your Dreams Away

FRANK SINATRA SINGS FOR ONLY THE LONEY
Capitol SW 1053
Arranged and conducted by Nelson Riddle

Only The Lonely
Angel Eyes
What's New?
It's A Lonesome Old Town
Willow Weep For Me
Goodbye
Blues In The Night
Guess I'll Hang My Tears Out To Dry
Ebb Tide
Spring Is Here
Gone With The Wind
One For My Baby

NOTE: The original stereo issue did not include 'It's A Lonesome Old Town' and 'Spring Is Here'.

COME FLY WITH ME
Capitol SW 920
Arranged and conducted by Billy May

Come Fly With Me
Around The World
Isle of Capri
Moonlight In Vermont
Autumn In New York
On The Road To Mandalay
Let's Get Away From It All
April In Paris
London By Night
Brazil
Blue Hawaii
It's Nice To Go Trav'lin'

NOTE: Because of copyright problems, 'On The Road To Mandalay' did not appear on British releases. On the mono version, it was replaced by 'It Happened In Monterey' and on the stereo version by 'French Foreign Legion'.

COME DANCE WITH ME
Capitol SW 1069
Arranged and conducted by Billy May

Come Dance With Me
Something's Gotta Give
Just In Time
Dancing In The Dark
Too Close For Comfort
I Could Have Danced All Night
Saturday Night
Day In Day Out
Cheek To Cheek
Baubles, Bangles And Beads
The Song Is You
The Last Dance

COME SWING WITH ME
Capitol SW 1594
Arranged by Heinie Beau and Billy May and conducted by Billy May

Day By Day
Sentimental Journey
Almost Like Being In Love
Five Minutes More
American Beauty Rose
Yes Indeed
The Sunny Side of The Street
Don't Take Your Love From Me
That Old Black Magic
Lover
Paper Doll
I've Heard That Song Before

NO ONE CARES
Capitol SW 1221
Arranged and conducted by Gordon Jenkins

When No One Cares
A Cottage For Sale
Stormy Weather
Where Do You Go?
A Ghost of a Chance
Here's That Rainy Day
I Can't Get Started
Why Try To Change Me Now?
Just Friends
I'll Never Smile Again
None But The Lonely Heart

LOOK TO YOUR HEART
Capitol 1164
Arranged and conducted by Nelson Riddle, except 'I'm Gonna Live'

Look To Your Heart
Anytime, Anywhere
Not As A Stranger
Our Town
You, My Love
Same Old Saturday Night
Fairy Tale

The Impatient Years
I Could Have Told You
When I Stop Loving You
If I Had Three Wishes
I'm Gonna Live Till I Die

NICE 'N' EASY
Capitol 1417
Arranged and conducted by Nelson Riddle

Nice 'N' Easy
That Old Feeling
How Deep Is The Ocean?
I've Got A Crush On You
You Go To My Head
Fools Rush In
Nevertheless
She's Funny That Way
Try A Little Tenderness
Embraceable You
Mam'selle
Dream

SWING EASY
Capitol 1429
Arranged and conducted by Nelson Riddle, except 'Lean Baby'

Jeepers Creepers
Taking A Chance On Love
Wrap Your Troubles In Dreams
Lean Baby
I Love You
I'm Gonna Sit Right Down And Write Myself A Letter
Get Happy
All Of Me
How Could You Do A Thing Like That To Me?
Why Should I Cry Over You?
Sunday
Just One of Those Things

ALL THE WAY
Capitol SW 1538
Arranged and conducted by Nelson Riddle

High Hopes
Talk To Me
French Foreign Legion
To Love And Be Loved
River Stay 'Way From My Door
All The Way
It's Over, It's Over, It's Over
Ol' MacDonald
This Was My Love
All My Tomorrows
Sleep Warm
Witchcraft

SINATRA'S SWINGING SESSION
Capitol SW 1491
Arranged and conducted by Nelson Riddle

When You're Smiling
Blue Moon
S'posin'
It All Depends On You
It's Only A Paper Moon
My Blue Heaven
Should I?
September In The Rain
Always
I Can't Believe That You're In Love With Me
I Concentrate On You
You Do Something To Me

POINT OF NO RETURN
Capitol SW 1676
Arranged by Heinie Beau and Axel

Stordahl, and conducted by Axel Stordahl

When The World Was Young
I'll Remember April
September Song
A Million Dreams Ago
I'll See You Again
There Will Never Be Another You
Somewhere Along The Way
It's A Blue World
These Foolish Things
As Time Goes By
I'll Be Seeing You
Memories of You

A JOLLY CHRISTMAS FROM FRANK SINATRA
Capitol W 894
Arranged and conducted by Gordon Jenkins, with the Ralph Brewster Singers

Jingle Bells
The Christmas Song
Mistletoe And Holly
I'll Be Home For Christmas
The Christmas Waltz
Have Yourself A Merry Little Christmas
The First Noël
Hark, The Herald Angels Sing
O Little Town of Bethlehem
Adeste Fideles
It Came Upon A Midnight Clear
Silent Night

Reprise

RING-A-DING DING!
Reprise FS 1001
Arranged and conducted by Johnny Mandel

Ring-A-Ding Ding
Let's Fall In Love
Be Careful, It's My Heart
A Foggy Day
A Fine Romance
In The Still Of The Night
The Coffee Song
When I Take My Sugar To Tea
Let's Face The Music And Dance
I've Got My Love To Keep Me Warm

SINATRA SWINGS
Reprise FS 1002
Arranged and conducted by Billy May

Falling In Love With Love
The Curse Of An Aching Heart
Don't Cry, Joe
Please Don't Talk About Me When I'm Gone
Love Walked In
Granada
I Never Knew
Don't Be That Way
Moonlight On The Ganges
It's A Wonderful World
Have You Met Miss Jones?
You're Nobody Till Somebody Loves You

I REMEMBER TOMMY . . .
Reprise FS 1003
Arranged and conducted by Sy Oliver

I'm Getting Sentimental Over You
Imagination
There Are Such Things
East Of The Sun
Daybreak

Without A Song
I'll Be Seeing You
Take Me
It's Always You
Polka Dots And Moonbeams
It Started All Over Again
The One I Love Belongs To Somebody Else (with Sy Oliver)
I'm Getting Sentimental Over You (edited)

SINATRA AND STRINGS
Reprise FS 1004
Arranged and conducted by Don Costa

I Hadn't Anyone Till You
Night And Day
Misty
Stardust
Come Rain Or Come Shine
It Might As Well Be Spring
Prisoner Of Love
That's All
All Or Nothing At All
Yesterdays

SINATRA AND SWINGIN' BRASS
Reprise FS 1005
Arranged and conducted by Neal Hefti

Goody Goody
They Can't Take That Away From Me
At Long Last Love
I'm Beginning To See The Light
Don'cha Go 'Way Mad
I Get A Kick Out Of You
Tangerine
Love Is Just Around The Corner
Ain't She Sweet
Serenade In Blue
I Love You
Pick Yourself Up

SINATRA SINGS SONGS FROM GREAT BRITAIN
Reprise R9 1006
Arranged and conducted by Robert Farnon

The Very Thought Of You
We'll Gather Lilacs
If I Had You
Now Is The Hour
Gypsy
A Nightingale Sang In Berkeley Square
A Garden In The Rain
London By Night
We'll Meet Again
I'll Follow My Secret Heart

NOTE: The only LP recorded outside the US.

ALL ALONE
Reprise FS 1007
Arranged and conducted by Gordon Jenkins

All Alone
The Girl Next Door
Are You Lonesome Tonight?
Charmaine
What'll I Do?
When I Lost You
Oh, How I Miss You Tonight
Indiscreet
Remember
Together
The Song Is Ended

SINATRA-BASIE
Reprise FS 1008
Arranged and conducted by Neal Hefti

Pennies From Heaven

Please Be Kind
The Tender Trap
Looking At The World Through Rose Coloured Glasses
My Kind Of Girl
I Only Have Eyes For You
Nice Work If You Can Get It
Learnin' The Blues
I'm Gonna Sit Right Down And Write Myself A Letter
I Won't Dance

THE CONCERT SINATRA
Reprise FS 1009
Arranged and conducted by Nelson Riddle

I Have Dreamed
My Heart Stood Still
Lost In The Stars
Ol' Man River
You'll Never Walk Alone
Bewitched
This Nearly Was Mine
Soliloquy

SINATRA'S SINATRA
Reprise FS 1010
Arranged and conducted by Nelson Riddle

I've Got You Under My Skin
In The Wee Small Hours Of The Morning
The Second Time Around
Nancy
Witchcraft
Young At Heart
All The Way
How Little We Know
Pocketful of Miracles
Oh, What It Seemed To Be
Call Me Irresponsible
Put Your Dreams Away

FRANK SINATRA SINGS DAYS OF WINE AND ROSES
Reprise FS 1011
Arranged and conducted by Nelson Riddle

Days Of Wine And Roses
Moon River
The Way You Look Tonight
Three Coins In The Fountain
In the Cool Cool Cool Of The Evening
Secret Love
Swinging On A Star
It Might As Well Be Spring
The Continental
Love Is A Many Splendoured Thing
All The Way

IT MIGHT AS WELL BE SWING
Reprise FS 1012
Arranged and conducted by Quincy Jones

Fly Me To The Moon
I Wish You Love
I Believe In You
More
I Can't Stop Loving You
Hello Dolly
I Wanna Be Around
The Best Is Yet To Come
The Good Life
Wives And Lovers

SOFTLY AS I LEAVE YOU
Reprise FS 1013
With various arrangers and conductors

Emily
Here's To The Losers

Dear Heart
Come Blow Your Horn
Love Isn't Just For The Young
I Can't Believe I'm Losing You
Pass Me By
Softly As I Leave You
Then Suddenly Love
Available
Talk To Me, Baby
The Look Of Love

SEPTEMBER OF MY YEARS
Reprise FS 1014
*Arranged and conducted by Gordon
Jenkins*

The September Of My Years
How Old Am I?
Don't Wait Too Long
It Gets Lonely Early
This Is All I Ask
Last Night When We Were Young
The Man In The Looking Glass
It Was A Very Good Year
When The Wind Was Green
Hello, Young Lovers
I See It Now
Once Upon A Time
September Song

MY KIND OF BROADWAY
Reprise FS 1015
With various arrangers and conductors

Ev'rybody Has The Right To Be Wrong
Golden Moment
Luck Be A Lady
Lost In The Stars
Hello, Dolly
I'll Only Miss Her When I Think Of
    Her
They Can't Take That Away From Me
Yesterdays
Nice Work If You Can Get It
Have You Met Miss Jones?
Without A Song

SINATRA: A MAN AND HIS MUSIC
Reprise 2FS 1016
With various arrangers and conductors

Put Your Dreams Away
All Or Nothing At All
I'll Never Smile Again
There Are Such Things
I'll Be Seeing You
The One I Love Belongs To Somebody
    Else
Polka Dots And Moonbeams
Night And Day
Oh, What It Seemed To Be
Soliloquy
Nancy
The House I Live In
Extract from *From Here To Eternity*
Come Fly With Me
How Little We Know
Learnin' The Blues
In The Wee Small Hours Of The
    Morning
Young At Heart
Witchcraft
All The Way
Love And Marriage
I've Got You Under My Skin
Ring-A-Ding Ding
The Second Time Around
The Summit (with Dean Martin et al)
The Oldest Established (with
    Bing Crosby et al)
Luck Be A Lady
Call Me Irresponsible
Fly Me To The Moon
Softly As I Leave You

My Kind Of Town
The September Of My Years

NOTE: This is the double album made
for his fiftieth birthday.

STRANGERS IN THE NIGHT
Reprise FS 1017
*Arranged and conducted by Nelson
Riddle, except for the title song*

Strangers In The Night
Summer Wind
All Or Nothing At All
Call Me
You're Driving Me Crazy
On A Clear Day
My Baby Just Cares For Me
Downtown
Yes, Sir, That's My Baby
The Most Beautiful Girl In The World

MOONLIGHT SINATRA
Reprise FS 1018
*Arranged and conducted by Nelson
Riddle*

Moonlight Becomes You
Moon Song
Moonlight Serenade
Reaching For The Moon
I Wished On The Moon
Oh, You Crazy Moon
The Moon Got In My Eyes
Moonlight Mood
Moon Love
The Moon Was Yellow

SINATRA AT THE SANDS
Reprise 2FS 1019
*In concert with Count Basie and his
Orchestra*

Come Fly With Me
I've Got A Crush On You
I've Got You Under My Skin
The Shadow Of Your Smile
Street Of Dreams
One For My Baby
Fly Me To The Moon
One O'Clock Jump (instrumental)
Monologue
You Make Me Feel So Young
All Of Me (instrumental)
The September Of My Years
Get Me To The Church On Time
It Was A Very Good Year
Don't Worry 'Bout Me
Makin' Whoopee (instrumental)
Where Or When?
Angel Eyes
My Kind Of Town
Monologue
My Kind Of Town (reprise)

NOTE: This is a double album.

THAT'S LIFE
Reprise FS 1020
*Arranged and conducted by Ernie
Freeman*

That's Life
I Will Wait For You
Somewhere My Love
Sand And Sea
What Now My Love?
Winchester Cathedral
Give Her Love
Tell Her You Love Her Each Day
The Impossible Dream
You're Gonna Hear From Me

FRANCIS ALBERT SINATRA AND ANTONIO CARLOS JOBIM
Reprise FS 1021
*Arranged and conducted by Claus
Ogerman*

The Girl From Ipanema (with Antonio
    Carlos Jobim)
Dindi
Change Partners
Quiet Nights Of Quiet Stars
Meditation
If You Never Come To Me
How Insensitive (with Antonio Carlos
    Jobim)
I Concentrate On You (with Antonio
    Carlos Jobim)
Baubles, Bangles And Beads (with
    Antonio Carlos Jobim)
Once I Loved

FRANK SINATRA AND THE WORLD WE KNEW
Reprise FS 1022
With various arrangers and conductors

The World We Knew
Somethin' Stupid (with Nancy Sinatra)
This Is My Love
Born Free
Don't Sleep In The Subway
This Town
This Is My Song
You Are There
Drinking Again
Some Enchanted Evening

THE SINATRA CHRISTMAS ALBUM
Reprise FS 1023

The sleeve for this album was designed
but the album was never recorded.

FRANCIS A. AND EDWARD K.
Reprise FS 1024
*Arranged by Billy May, with the Duke
Ellington Orchestra*

Follow Me
Sunny
All I Need Is The Girl
Indian Summer
I Like The Sunrise
Yellow Days
Poor Butterfly
Come Back To Me

FRANK SINATRA'S GREATEST HITS!
Reprise FS 1025
With various arrangers and conductors

Strangers In The Night
Summer Wind
It Was A Very Good Year
Somewhere In Your Heart
Forget Domani
Somethin' Stupid (with Nancy Sinatra)
That's Life
Tell Her You Love Her Each Day
When Somebody Loves You
This Town
Softly As I Leave You

THE SINATRA FAMILY WISH YOU A HAPPY CHRISTMAS
Reprise FS 1026
*Arranged and conducted by Nelson
Riddle, except for 'Whatever Happened
To Christmas?'*

I Wouldn't Trade Christmas (with the
    rest of family)
It's Such A Lonely Time Of Year

(Nancy Jr)
Some Children See Him (Frank Jr)
O Bambino (Tina and Nancy Jr)
The Bells of Christmas (with rest of family)
Whatever Happened To Christmas?
Santa Claus Is Coming To Town (Tina)
Kids (Nancy Jr)
The Christmas Waltz
The Twelve Days of Christmas (with rest of family)

CYCLES
Reprise FS 1027
Arranged by Don Costa and conducted by Bill Miller

Rain In My Heart
From Both Sides Now
Little Green Apples
Pretty Colours
Cycles
Wandering
By The Time I Get To Phoenix
Moody River
My Way of Life
Gentle On My Mind

MY WAY
Reprise FS 1029
Arranged and conducted by Don Costa

Watch What Happens
Didn't We?
Hallelujah I Love Her So
Yesterday
All My Tomorrows
My Way
A Day In The Life of A Fool
For Once In My Life
If You Go Away
Mrs Robinson

A MAN ALONE
Reprise FS 1030
Arranged and conducted by Don Costa

A Man Alone
Night
I've Been To Town
From Promise To Promise
The Single Man
The Beautiful Strangers
Lonesome Cities
Love's Been Good To Me
Empty Is
Out Beyond The Window
Some Travelling Music
A Man Alone (reprise)

WATERTOWN
Reprise FS 1031
With various arrangers and conductors

Watertown
Goodbye
For A While
Michael And Peter
I Would Be In Love Anyway
Elizabeth
What A Funny Girl You Used To Be
What's Now Is Now
She Says
The Train

FRANK SINATRA'S GREATEST HITS, VOLUME II
Reprise FS 1032
With various arrangers and conductors

The Shadow Of Your Smile
Yesterday
Blue Lace
For Once In My Life
Born Free

My Way
Little Green Apples
From Both Sides Now
Mrs Robinson
Call Me Irresponsible
Gentle On My Mind
Love's Been Good To Me

NOTE: This LP has been released in virtually every country except the US.

SINATRA AND COMPANY
Reprise FS 1033
With various arrangers and conductors

Drinking Water (with Antonio Carlos Jobim)
Someone To Light Up My Life
Triste
Don't Ever Go Away
This Happy Madness (with Antonio Carlos Jobim)
Wave
One Note Samba (with Antonio Carlos Jobim)
I Will Drink The Wine
Close To You
Sunrise In The Morning
Bein' Green
My Sweet Lady
Leaving On A Jet Plane
Lady Day

HAVE YOURSELF A MERRY LITTLE CHRISTMAS
Reprise R 50001
With various arrangers and conductors

Have Yourself A Merry Little Christmas
O Little Town Of Bethlehem (Jo Stafford)
A Vision of Sugar Plums (Billy May)
What Child Is This? (The McGuire Sisters)
The First Noël (Keely Smith)
Deck The Halls (The Hi-Lo's)
Jingle Bells (Sammy Davis Jr)
Christmas Medley (Les Baxter's Balladeers)
Christmas Medley (Mavis Rivers)
Adeste Fideles (Lou Monte)
Cantique de Noel (Nelson Riddle)
It Came Upon The Midnight Clear (Rosemary Clooney)
Christmas Medley (Dean Martin)

SINATRA '65
Reprise R9 6167
With various arrangers and conductors

Tell Her You Love Her Each Day
Anytime At All
Stay With Me
I Like To Lead When I Dance
You Brought A New Kind Of Love To Me
My Kind Of Town
When Somebody Loves You
Somewhere In Your Heart
I've Never Been In Love Before
When I'm Not Near The Girl I Love
Luck Be A Lady

OL' BLUE EYES IS BACK
Reprise FS 2155
Arranged by Don Costa and Gordon Jenkins and conducted by Gordon Jenkins

You Will Be My Music
You're So Right
Winners
Nobody Wins
Send In The Clowns

Dream Away
Let Me Try Again
There Used To Be A Ballpark
Noah

NOTE: This was the comeback LP.

SOME NICE THINGS I'VE MISSED
Reprise FS 2195
Arranged by Don Costa and Gordon Jenkins

You Turned My World Around
Sweet Caroline
The Summer Knows
I'm Gonna Make It All The Way
Tie A Yellow Ribbon Round The Ole Oak Tree
Satisfy Me One More Time
If
You Are The Sunshine Of My Life
What Are You Doing The Rest Of Your Life?
Bad Bad Leroy Brown

SINATRA–THE MAIN EVENT
Reprise FS 2207
In concert with Woody Herman and the Young Thundering Herd

The Lady Is A Tramp
I Get A Kick Out Of You
Let Me Try Again
Autumn In New York
I've Got You Under My Skin
Bad Bad Leroy Brown
Angel Eyes
You Are The Sunshine Of My Life
The House I Live In
My Kind Of Town
My Way

Early Sinatra

With Harry James

From The Bottom Of My Heart (13/7/39)
Melancholy Mood (13/7/39)
It's Funny To Everyone But Me (17/8/39)
Here Comes The Night (17/9/39)
All Or Nothing At All (17/9/39)
On A Little Street In Singapore (13/10/39)
Who Told You I Cared? (13/10/39)
Ciribiribin (8/11/39)
Every Day Of My Life (8/11/39)

NOTE: These are the only commercial recordings Sinatra made with James.

With Tommy Dorsey

THE DORSEY/SINATRA SESSIONS 1940–1942
RCA Victor SD 1000

The Sky Fell Down
Too Romantic
Shake Down The Stars
Moments In The Moonlight
I'll Be Seeing You
Say It
Polka Dots And Moonbeams
The Fable Of The Rose
This Is The Beginning Of The End
Hear My Song, Violetta
Fools Rush In
Devil May Care
April Played The Fiddle
I Haven't Time To Be A Millionaire

Imagination
Yours Is My Heart Alone
You're Lonely And I'm Lonely
East Of The Sun (with band chorus)
Head On My Pillow
It's A Lovely Day Tomorrow
I'll Never Smile Again (with the Pied Pipers)
All This And Heaven Too
Where Do You Keep Your Heart?
Whispering (with the Pied Pipers)
Trade Winds
The One I Love (with the Pied Pipers)
The Call Of The Canyon
Love Lies
I Could Make You Care
The World Is In My Arms
Our Love Affair
Looking For Yesterday
Tell Me At Midnight
We Three
When You Awake
Anything
Shadows On The Sand
You're Breaking My Heart All Over Again
I'd Know You Anywhere
Do You Know Why?
Not So Long Ago
Stardust (with the Pied Pipers)
You Lucky People, You
It's Always You
I Tried
Dolores (with the Pied Pipers)
Without A Song
Do I Worry? (with the Pied Pipers)
Everything Happens To Me
Let's Get Away From It All (with the Pied Pipers)
I'll Never Let A Day Pass By
Love Me As I Am
This Love Of Mine
I Guess I'll Have To Dream The Rest (with the Pied Pipers)
You And I
Neiani (with the Pied Pipers)
Free For All (with the Pied Pipers)
Blue Skies (with band chorus)
Two In Love
Pale Moon
I Think Of You
How Do You Do Without Me?
A Sinner Kissed An Angel
Violets For Your Furs
The Sunshine Of Your Smile
How About You?
Snooty Little Cutie (with the Pied Pipers)
Poor You
I'll Take Tallulah (with the Pied Pipers)
The Last Call For Love (with the Pied Pipers)
Somewhere A Voice Is Calling
Just As Though You Were Here (with the Pied Pipers)
Street of Dreams (with the Pied Pipers)
Take Me
Be Careful, It's My Heart (with the Pied Pipers)
In The Blue Of The Evening
Dig Down Deep (with the Pied Pipers)
There Are Such Things (with the Pied Pipers)
Daybreak
It Started All Over Again (with the Pied Pipers)
Light A Candle In The Chapel

NOTE: This is a six LP boxed set.

Acknowledgments

People

My sincere thanks go to the many people who have given me time, information and material, in particular David Quinlan, Anne Flemming, Ken Thompson, and Tony Morrison. As always, I owe an immense debt of gratitude to my wife Maggie, who not only gave me inspiration and encouragement when I needed them but also compiled the index.

Very special thanks are due to Beryl Overbury of the Sinatra Music Society and to John Ridgway, author of *The Sinatrafile*. Quite simply, without their assistance, this book would have been incomplete.

Finally, my grateful thanks to all at Hamlyns who have been involved with this book: if a writer is to have a conscience— and it is essential that he should—I can think of no better way to get one than from the gentle prodding and immense help I have received from this quarter.

Sources

Grateful acknowledgment is made to the critics, authors, and journalists who are quoted in this book–also to their publishers. The newspapers, periodicals, and magazines that have been helpful are: Daily Express, Daily Herald, Daily Mail, Daily Mirror, Daily Sketch, Daily Telegraph, Esquire, Evening News, Evening Standard, Film Review, Films and Filming, The Guardian, The Hollywood Reporter, Life, Melody Maker, Modern Screen, News Chronicle, News of the World, Newsweek, The Observer, Photoplay, Picture Show, Radio Guide, Reveille, Reynolds News, Rolling Stone, The Sun, The Sunday Express, Sunday Mirror, Sunday Telegraph, Sunday Times, Time, The Times, TV Guide, TV Times, Variety, and Woman.

The books that were used include:
Capra, Frank: *The Name Above the Title.* Collier Macmillan, New York, 1971.
Douglas-Home, Robin: *Sinatra.* Michael Joseph, London, 1962. Grosset & Dunlap, New York, 1963.
Eames, John D.: *The MGM Story.* Crown, New York, 1975. Octopus, London, 1975.
Fordin, Hugh: *The World of Entertainment.* Doubleday, New York, 1975.
Frank, Gerold: *Judy.* Harper & Row, New York, and W. H. Allen, London, 1975.
Goodman, Ezra: *The Fifty-Year Decline and Fall of Hollywood.* Simon & Schuster, New York, 1961.
Gow, Gordon: *Hollywood in the Fifties.* Zwemmer, London, and A. S. Barnes, New York, 1971.
Hamblett, Charles: *The Hollywood Cage.* Hart, New York, 1970.
Higham, Charles: *Ava.* Delacorte, New York, 1974. W. H. Allen, London, 1975.
Higham, Charles and Joel Greenberg: *Hollywood in the Forties.* Zwemmer, London, and A. S. Barnes, New York. 1968.
Kahn Jr, E. J.: *The Voice.* Musicians Press, London, 1946.
Ridgway, John: *The Sinatrafile* (Parts 1 and 2). Ridgway Books, Birmingham, England, 1977.
Ringgold, Gene and Clifford McCarty: *The Films of Frank Sinatra.* Citadel Press, New York, 1971.
Romero, Jerry: *Sinatra's Women.* Manor Books, New York, 1975.
Scaduto, Tony: *Frank Sinatra.* Michael Joseph, London, and Pinnacle Books, New York, 1976 (under the pseudonym Tony Sciacca).
Shaper, Hal: *Sinatra: The Man and His Music.* Wise Publications, London, 1975.
Shaw, Arnold: *Sinatra.* Holt, Rinehart & Winston, New York, and W. H. Allen, London, 1968.
Springer, John: *All Singing! All Talking! All Dancing!* Citadel Press, New York, 1970.
Thomas, Bob: *King Cohn.* Putnam, New York, and Barrie and Rockliff, London, 1967.
Wilson, Earl: *The Show Business Nobody Knows.* W. H. Allen, London, 1972. US title: *Show Business Laid Bare.* Putnam, New York, 1974.
Wilson, Earl: *Sinatra.* W. H. Allen, London, and Collier Macmillan, New York, 1976.

Photographs

Colour Camera Press, London: John Bryson 143, 144, Robin Douglas-Home 53 top, Ray Johnson 144 inset, Terry O'Neill 71; Cinema Bookshop, London 35; Joel Finler, London 126 top; Metro-Goldwyn-Mayer 18; Pictorial Press, London 108, 125; Rex Features, London 36, 89, 107, 126 bottom; Time Inc. 36 inset, 72; Warner Bros. 17, 53 bottom, 54, 90.

Black and white Associated Press, London 41 bottom, 56, 64 top, 113 bottom, 116, 119 right, 141 top and bottom, 164 top left; Camera Press, London 11, 13 top, 50 bottom, 62, 104, 114-115, 123, 133, 135 bottom; Capitol Records 82 top; Cinema Bookshop, London 79 top, 162 bottom, 165 top right, 168 bottom left; Columbia 157 top; Culver Pictures, New York 23, 41 centre, 42, 48, 154 top; Joel Finler, London 59, 160 top; Globe Photos, New York 77, 81 bottom right; Hamlyn Group Picture Library 28 top, 96 top, 102-103, 152 centre, 154 centre, 161 top left, 167 top left; Hamlyn Group: Cecil Reilly Associates 25 top left, 31 top left, 49 right, 113 top right, John Webb 43 bottom right, 50 top and centre, 58 inset, 81 top right, 120 right, 137 top, 138 right; Keystone Press Agency, London 129 bottom, 130 bottom, 131 right, 137 bottom, 146 right, 150, 151; Kobal Collection, London 44, 47 top left, 69 top, 98, 156 bottom, 157 bottom left; Metro-Goldwyn-Mayer 8 right, 93 bottom, 97, 155 bottom right, 159 bottom right, 161 bottom; National Film Archive, London 93 top, 96 bottom, 152 top, 155 top and bottom left, 156 top left, 157 bottom right, 158 centre and bottom, 159 top and bottom left, 160 centre, 168 right; The New Yorker 12, 21 left, 46 right, 47 right, 49 left, 61 top; New York Times endpapers, 41 top; Beryl Overbury, Redditch 31 bottom left, 39 top; Paramount 164 right; Penguin Photo, New York 14, 15, 27, 28 bottom, 30, 33 top and bottom, 39 bottom, 40, 57 bottom, 94 top right, 152 bottom; Pictorial Parade, New York 7, 13, 20, 31 right, 58, 61 bottom, 75, 86 bottom, 111 bottom; Pictorial Press, London 9, 43 left, 45 left, 51, 64 bottom, 84 top, 86 top, 98, 99 top right and bottom right, 100, 101 top, 111 top, 115 top, 118-119, 119 bottom left, 121, 132 bottom, 140 bottom, 162 top left, 163 right; Popperfoto, London 1, 8 left, 21 right, 43 top right, 65, 66 top, bottom left and bottom right, 68, 69 bottom, 81 left, 87, 94 top left and bottom, 95, 115 bottom, 131 left, 146 left, 147 bottom, 148, 153 bottom, 167 top left; Radio Times Hulton Picture Library, London 76; Rex Features, London 2-3, 4-5, 80, 83, 84 bottom, 84-85, 105, 117 top and bottom, 122, 129 top left and top right, 132 top, 138 left, 140 top, 147 top, 166 top left, 167 bottom, 168 top left; Syndication International, London 24-25, 25 top right, 47 bottom left, 57 top, 63 top and bottom, 79 bottom left and bottom right, 82 bottom, 92, 101 bottom, 112, 120 left, 135 top, 149, 153 centre, 154 bottom, 156 top right, 160 bottom, 162 top right, 163 bottom, 164 bottom left; Time Inc. 110, 113 top left, 128, 134 left and right, 139; United Artists 158 top, 161 top right, 166 right; Warner Bros. 163 top left, 165 left and bottom right, 166 bottom left; Warner/Elektra/Atlantic 10.

Index